# Off-Road Nirvana: Finding the Top 100+ Trails in the Rocky Mountains

**An Ultimate Bucket List of 4X4 Trails in Arizona, Colorado, Idaho, Montana, Nevada, New Mexico, Utah, and Wyoming.**

## Steven Lee

# Dedication

To my wife Merry, who has stood by me and put up with crazy ideas, dreams, and travels.

To my four blonde adventurous daughters; Jennifer, Jessica, Aubrey, & Megan, who constantly remind me how fun life can be off the beaten path.

# Table of Contents

# QR Codes For Mapping Trailheads

In this book we have provided QR codes for each trail's trailhead so it is always quickly available for your travels via Google Maps. The QR codes not only provide you with coordinates to the location, but also pictures of the area. You never have to wander about looking for the trailhead, we will get you there quickly and easily.

If you're reading the book digitally online, or if you have the printed version, you can easily use your phone's camera to scan the QR code. We also provide the physical coordinates If you prefer to enter it into your GPS manually.

As an example, here is the QR code for Hell's Revenge trailhead near Moab, Utah. Feel free to give it a try.

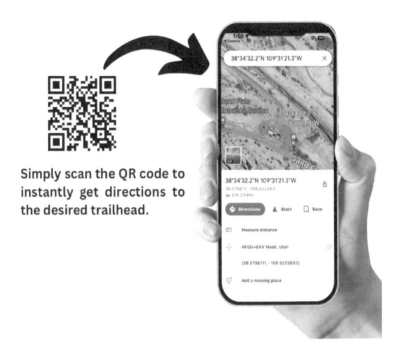

Simply scan the QR code to instantly get directions to the desired trailhead.

Trailhead Coordinates: 38.575360, -109.522870

# Free Gifts

Use this next QR code to Register for our monthly FREE GIFTS giveaways and/or download any of our FREE publications, including our kid's off-road coloring book to keep them busy on the way to your next ride!

# Preface

"In every walk with nature, one receives far more than he seeks." - John Muir

Ah, the great outdoors - a place where Wi-Fi is weak, but the connection to backcountry beauty is strong. In this realm of dirt and sky, it's easy to feel both infinitely small and still part of something grand, which is exactly how I feel every time my somewhat deflated tires roll onto a new trail that I have not driven before. That joy of finding and taking on new trails is what has led me to write down what I've learned about taking on these challenging terrains, as well as providing trails that I believe you will enjoy.

**Welcome to your guide to finding and understanding the top 100+ trails in the Rocky Mountain West.**

You may be asking, why this book? Well, let's take a step back. By day, I produce feature films and TV series that have stories that I hope to enchant, entertain, and sometimes even educate my viewers. But once the director calls 'that's a wrap', you'll find me swapping my days on set dealing with production schedules, budgets, and meetings for steering wheels and deflated tires, as I dive headfirst into some new 4-wheel trail that, as my wife says, I have no business attempting at my age—yes, I am over fifty, and we will leave it at that.

This dual life has taught me one thing - the joy of exploration is found not just in reaching your destination but in the fun, humor, and learning that comes with every bump along the journey.

I've seen firsthand eager drivers heading into the wilderness, their spirits high but their preparedness, well, taking a bit of a backseat–and yes, I have been guilty of this myself. There has been more than once I have confused a riverbed with a shortcut; or I thought 'all-terrain' tires meant lunar surfaces were fair game. As I have talked with some other off-road enthusiasts, I have found that more than a few share a common thread; a deep love for the wild yet a slight oversight in the preparedness department. If you ever watch Matt's Off Road Recovery videos, you will see what I mean.

So combining my experiences with other rider's stories, insights, and yes, mishaps, became the spark plugs behind my motivation to shift gears and write this book.

## Inspirations and the Road Less Traveled

Much like a movie, this book wouldn't have been possible without a stellar cast supporting it from behind the scenes. From seasoned off-roaders who have stopped me on the trail and imparted some important wisdom, to the rangers and other land-management specialists who ensure these trails can be enjoyed by generations to come, I want to offer my heartfelt thanks. And most importantly, to my amazing wife, who puts up with my wanderlust, and tolerates my incessant rambling about our next ride. All of their support helps fuel my drive, both literally and metaphorically.

## To You, The Readers

Choosing to spend your time with this book means you're ready to dive headfirst into the rugged beauty of the Mountain West, and for that, I both salute and thank you. Whether you're a seasoned off-roader looking for the next big challenge or someone who's just swapped their sedan for a 4x4, there's something in here for you. Armed with a little humor and a shared desire for adventure, we will review the rules for off-road safety, gain a better understanding of the digital compasses that will help lead us along our trails and back again, and most importantly, we will find exciting new trails that you have probably not heard of, leave alone driven.

Expect to finish these pages with dirt under your fingernails (figuratively, of course, unless you're reading while on the trail, then please watch out for that six-foot dropoff just around the next bend) and a newfound confidence in your ability to tackle any terrain. Think of this as your GPS to off-road fun and greater understanding; from finding exciting new trails to getting great tips on how to keep your four-wheeled machine happy and running smooth.

Thank you for choosing to embark on this adventure with me. It's time to shift into gear, engage the 4WD, and let the journey to finding the top 100+ trails in the Mountain West begin.

## Two Sections For You

This book is divided into two sections.

1. Understanding your abilities, your vehicle, and the world you will be driving in

2. The top 100+ trails & trailways throughout the rocky mountain region

If you are a seasoned off-road driver, you will probably know much of what is found in Section #1, but hopefully there will be some important things that even you can learn from. Section #2 is the gold of this book, providing facts and insight into the top 100+ trails throughout the region. I have yet to find someone who has wrangled all the trails listed here. From easy, scenic trips to the hardest trails available, we are going to explore them all.

If you are new to this exciting sport, off-road drivers, sometimes called "Wheelers"(someone who drives a 4-wheel drive vehicle) are a community of people who love to take on the challenge of driving on roads that an average stock car cannot drive. Whether they are driving a Jeep, another SUV, an OHV or ATV, these people are modern cowboys/cowgirls that have traded a horse for horsepower. It is not only an exciting hobby, in some ways it becomes a lifestyle, and community of people who are known to work together to take on some of nature's most challenging obstacles.

## The Rocky Mountain Region

I was raised in the Rockies, and I still live here. It is also called the Rocky Mountain Region, the Intermountain Region, and so forth. And depending on who you ask, this region includes the eight states of Arizona, Colorado, Idaho, Montana, Nevada, New Mexico, Utah, and Wyoming. There are subregions that exist within the Rocky's which is how most people group the states, but for this book I have chosen to include the states in alphabetical order rather than by region.

# Chapter 1:

# Assessing the Terrain

Amidst the rugged beauty of Utah's southern desert with its red rock towers thrusting towards the pale blue sky, my wife and I were poised in a Polaris RZR at the trailhead, ready for another day of adventure.

The air was filled with the scent of sagebrush, and the low rumble of the RZR's engine resonated around me. Today was going to be a great day–except for one thing. I was unfamiliar with the trail we would be taking, and we did not even have my phone or a map (that being said, my wife often reminds me that I don't use the maps I do have).

Taking stock of my past experiences and my misguided belief that I could find our way without any help, we ventured off into the ragged road ahead of us. Deep inside I knew that I was about to engage in a dance with nature where missteps could be challenging. But my pride and ego took over as I drove away from the trailhead with a cockiness that would soon get me in trouble. The problem was that I overestimated my experience and underestimated the mountain that stood before us. I knew where we needed to end up, but figured that I could take an unmarked and little traveled trail to get where I wanted to be.

As we drove onto the sunbathed expanse of sand dunes, each one rolling like waves stilled in time, the dance began. I felt my skill and machine could harmonize to carve a path across this desert canvas. It wasn't the first time I had navigated a machine across a sea of sand and desert hills, and the engine's hum helped me feel invincible as I navigated our machine up a little traveled trail.

For you experienced drivers, I'm sure you have already counted at least two mistakes I had already made. But I was bound and determined that I could get us where we needed to go.

Eventually, we found ourselves creeping along a very narrow shelf trail with rocks tumbling down hundreds of feet beneath us as my tires slowly rolled along. My wife was terrified, and even though I acted as cool as a cucumber, cajoling her that I was in complete control, I silently knew that I had gotten us into a very bad situation.

As I crept along this steep, rocky, and precarious cliff trail, I was reminded of the importance of choosing a trail that matched both my skills and the vehicle's capabilities. The desert cares nothing about our human pride, it demands respect and rewards preparation.

As the sun began its settle on the horizon and cradled the cliffs in hues of gold and auburn, I truly began to appreciate how my lack of preparation and overconfidence had put our lives at risk.

Eventually, we found our way back down to the main road. Silently, I patted myself on the back, I had gotten us out without anyone or anything getting damaged or hurt. It was at that moment that my wife hit me in the arm with such emotion that it shocked me back into reality. "Don't **ever** do that to me again!" she declared.

It was then that I understood how crucial it is to plan properly and how risky this sport can be if improperly executed.

## Understanding the Trail Ratings System

In the world of off-roading in the US, there are a few basic things every off-road driver should know. Understanding trail markers and trail ratings should be part of your knowledge bank. Getting to know and understand these signs is crucial to traveling safely in the hinterlands.

## Know the Trail Signs

Both the Forest Service and the BLM use standard signs on motorized off-road paths. Up to eight symbols can be used in one of three different ways on these signs. If there is a red slash through a symbol indicates that usage of the trail is prohibited. The dates of any seasonal closures for a trail may also be listed on the sign.

### Trailhead Sign

This type of sign includes all the signs erected at the trailhead to advise riders to ride safely, sensibly, and legally as well as to make the most of their recreational

experience fall under this category. Trailhead signs usually include a map. These maps are often in the form of a diagram. These maps often include trail layout, with a "You are here" notation, plus difficulty ratings, type (road, ATV, single track), use restrictions, points of interest, approximate segment lengths, service locations, major landmarks, and more. Trailhead signs often also include rules or laws governing the use of that specific trail, and emergency telephone numbers.

**Intersection Markers**

These are usually found on a vertical sign or post. They usually have reflective stickers on a brown flexible fiberglass pillar to create the vertical sign. These signs are common at trailheads and crossroads. These markers usually include the name, number, and/or trail symbol, difficulty rating, and directional arrows to indicate the trail direction. A red diagonal slash through a specific vehicle denotes restrictions for vehicle type or size.

A full size SUV will not fit on a trail meant for ATVs or narrow side-by-sides. Trying to run a trail that is too narrow for your vehicle will not only ruin your paint job, you ruin the trail for others.

## The Color Symbols System

Many trail markers will have a colored symbol on the signs. These symbols are similar to those found at ski resorts.

### Green Circle (easy)

- The best-developed pathways (nearly roads) with minimally steep hills and obstacles.
- Perfect for beginners who know how to ride safely on well-maintained routes.

### Blue Square (moderate)

- More challenging trails are narrower with steeper hills, switchbacks, and moderate barriers.

- Drivers with advanced capabilities who want a moderately difficult trail ride.
- Riders are at higher risk of danger and possible injury.

## Black Diamond (difficult)

- The most rudimentary trails require advanced abilities.
- Steep gradients, small pathways, acute alignments, hard footing, and large obstructions.
- Only for experienced riders to test their vehicles and skills.

**Orange Blazed** is reserved for motorcycle trails.

## The Numerical Rating System

The Colorado Association of 4 Wheel Drive Clubs, Inc. uses a numerical rating system from 1 through 10. This system has been adopted by many other states:

1. EASY: Rock or dirt road with possible rocks, sheer ledges, and waterfalls less than 6". Although possibly steep, traction is considered good. Most stock vehicles can easily drive these trails.

2. EASY: It is an easy dirt or rough road with possible rocks, tree trunks, vertical ledges, and waterfalls under 8" and 12" tall. Although possibly steep, traction is considered decent. Most AWD stock vehicles can easily drive these trails, and 2WD with decent clearance can usually handle these roads as well.

3. MODERATE: Rocky or undulated roads are common with rocks, tree trunks, sheer ledges, and waterfalls under 24". Tire placement becomes harder and is sometimes steep. These trails should not be driven in anything less than an AWD vehicle with decent clearance.

4. MODERATE: Rocky or undulated roads are common

with rocks, tree trunks, sheer ledges, and waterfalls under 36". Tire placement becomes harder and is steep and occasionally off-camber. AWD vehicles may or may not be able to handle these roads. It is recommended that stock 4WDs with decent clearance should be used.

5. DIFFICULT: Rocky or uneven conditions with rocks, tree trunks, sheer ledges, and waterfalls under 54". Tire placement becomes harder and is steep and more often off-camber. Nothing less than 4WDs or OHVs with good clearance, 4-low gearing, lockers are helpful, and good all-terrain tires should be used on these trails. Only experienced drivers should tackle these trails.

6. DIFFICULT: Rocky or uneven road conditions with possible rocks under 36" height, vertical ledges under 36", and waterfalls under 84". Tire placement becomes harder and is steep and often off-camber. Only custom 4WD or OHVs should be on these trails. They should have a winch, low-gearing, undercarriage protection, excellent all-terrain tires, lockers helpful, plenty of clearance, and an experienced driver at the helm.

7. VERY DIFFICULT: Very rocky or undulated road surface containing rocks with vertical ledges under 54" height or near waterfalls under 10' tall. Tire placement is often bad and is steep and often off-camber. Custom 4WD or OHVs should be the only ones to try these trails with an experienced driver. They should have a winch, low-gearing, undercarriage protection, excellent all-terrain tires, lockers are a must, and plenty of clearance.

8. SEVERE: Very rocky or undulated road surface. Rocks under 84" tall, vertical ledges under 72", and waterfalls under 14'. Bad tire placement and is steep and very often off-camber. Vehicle or bodily injury is possible. Necessities are a winch, low-gearing, undercarriage protection, excellent all-terrain tires, lockers, and plenty

of clearance.

9. SEVERE: Rocky or uneven road. Under 10' tall rocks. Vertical ledges under 8' tall or near waterfalls under 18'. Very bad tire placement and is steep and nearly always off-camber. Vehicle or bodily injury is quite possible.

10. EXTREME: Extremely rocky or uneven road, with rocks over-10'. Vertical ledges are above 8' high and waterfalls over 18'. Very bad tire placement and is steep and nearly always off-camber. Vehicle or bodily injury is highly possible. Only the very most experienced drivers or someone with a death wish should ever tackle these trails.

## A Second Numbering System

This is an overview of the Trail Ratings used as part of the OF4WD Trail Index. This numbering system only goes up to 5, but it actually is very similar to the system that goes from 1-10. It has a plus after each number; i.e. 1, 1+, 2, 2+, and so forth.

### 1 Maintained Dirt Roads

Throughout the year, these roads are maintained and graded. The water crossing depth is less than 3" inches, the bottom is hard, and it can normally be drivable with a 2-wheel drive car.

### 1+ Semi-Maintained Dirt Roads

These roads are occasionally graded, with very little maintenance. Drivers might go through sandy washes and washboards. If there is water, it is less than 3" deep. 2WD stock vehicles should be able to handle this road unless there is snow.

### 2 Easy 2WD/4WD

These are trails with obstacles that are simple to get around. When the weather is good, these roads might not need four-wheel drive (4WD) all the time. There will be ruts, washboarding, and water crossings up to 6 inches deep, as well as small rocks and holes.

## 2+ Easy 4WD

Roads with moderate difficulty that will necessitate 4WD. On these trails, you can come across a wide range of obstacles, including potholes, small washouts, water crossings up to 10 inches deep, medium-sized rocks, ruts and potholes. Off-road tires and increased ground clearance are advised. For stock cars, basic recovery equipment is advised (recovery strap)

## 3 Standard 4WD trail

These challenging trails call for 4WD. On these trails, you will face a range of more challenging obstacles, such as loose rocks, big potholes, water crossing depths up to 15", steep inclines up to 15 degrees, and larger rocks up to 10", as well as 8" mud-filled ruts. It is possible with a stock 4WD vehicle, but you should have traction devices like lockers, aggressive tires, and low air pressure. It is advisable to have ground clearance higher than stock. Low range gears are frequently utilized. You should have some experience and be able to drive well. Paint and/or rocker panel damage is possible. Recovering with straps or a hi-lift jack is advised.

## 3+ Challenging 4WD trail

These are tough roads that need low range 4WD. There are loose rocks, big holes, water crossings up to 20 inches, steep hills up to 20 degrees, and big rocks up to 12 inches deep in mud-filled ruts on these paths. It's not suggested to use a stock 4WD vehicle. It is highly suggested that the rear differential has a traction device (such as limited slip or lockers), aggressive tread, and low air pressure. Better than stock ground clearance is recommended. You should have some experience and be able to drive well. Paint and rocker panel damage is likely. Hi-lifts, straps, and winches are all recommended.

# 4 Difficult trail

Some of the rough terrain that these routes go through includes water crossings 24 inches or more, big rocks up to 15 inches in size, deep mud, steep hills, and side hills up to 30 degrees. A low-range 4WD system and more ground clearance than stock are needed. Low air pressure and aggressive tires are needed. Lift and bigger tires (33"+) are suggested, along with traction devices (Lockers or limited-slip) in the differentials (front and back). Off-road driving skills above average are needed on these roads. It may require more than one try to get past the hurdles. There could be damage to the paint, the body of the car, or the mechanics. Hi-lifts and winches are suggested.

## 4+ Severe trail

These trails go through very rough terrain with large boulders, very steep hills, and possible dangerous situations. For these trails, vehicles need to be modified with a lift, lockers, and tires that are 35.5 inches or bigger. You need to be very good at driving off-road. There's a chance of rolling over. There may be damage to the paint, the body of the car, or the mechanics. Winches are needed.

## 5 Extreme trail

These trails go through very rough terrain with large boulders, very steep hills, and possible dangerous situations. For these trails, vehicles need to be modified with a lift, lockers, and tires that are 35.5 inches or bigger. You need to be very good at driving off-road. There's a chance of rolling over. There will probably be damage to the paint, and also damage to the body or working parts of the vehicle. Winches are definitely needed.

## 5+ Impassable trail

Unless you are extremely well prepared, have a highly modified vehicle, and are very skilled at off-road driving, you should avoid these trails. There is the strong possibility for damage to the vehicle as well as personal injury. These trails should never be tackled alone.  On these trails drivers need a spotter, and possible rescue vehicles.

## Tread Lightly, Drive Hard

Let's start with the fact that off-road enthusiasts love the feel of unpaved ground under their tires. There's nothing quite like the anticipation of conquering a new trail as your machine growls when you push the gas pedal, eager to climb, crawl, and careen through Mother Nature's obstacle course. But hold your horsepower! Before you go channeling your inner rally driver, there's an essential to off-roading that you can't overlook: **trail assessment**.

Being able to assess the features of the terrain you're going to be riding on is an essential riding skill.  Consider your skill level when you review a trail, and be honest with your assessment of the trail and your experience.

There have been times when I have gone on a trail, and then returned to the same trail less than a week later to find that it had changed due to heavy rains in the area.  As an off-road rider, it is important for you to find out if there are any trail reports or issues that may have changed on your trail.

**Navigating the nuances of each terrain** is akin to knowing the difference between salsa and sriracha; both will add zest to your life, but one might just set your world on fire if you're not prepared.

Assessing trail difficulty is like a first date; first impressions matter, but it's the deeper conversation that reveals true compatibility. And let's be honest—your rig might make a great first impression with its shiny winch and beefy tires, but is it truly the perfect match for the rocky terrain or the enormous sand dunes ahead? Making the right choice is all about ensuring the vehicle, driver, and trail doesn't end in an unexpected breakup halfway up a mountain–or worse, down the side of a jagged cliff.

**Choosing a trail** that aligns with your skill level and your vehicle's capabilities is going to make for a much better experience for you and your passengers. Wise off-roaders know that a safe and enjoyable experience doesn't just happen; it's something that you earn by preparing properly, as well as picking the right vehicle for the terrain. Just like trying to take a full size Jeep on a trail made for OHVs under 50" in width. I may work, but there's going to be some damage along the way. Similarly, matching your skills with the proper trail difficulty ensures you don't bite off more than you or your trusty 4X4 can handle.

Throughout the pages that follow, I hope to provide you with lots of choices so that you can pick the trails that are best suited for you with your experience level, and the capacities of your vehicle.

I recently was in Moab on Hell's Revenge. At the bottom of the portion of the trail called Hell's Gate was a brand new stock Jeep Rubicon that had rolled back down the hill. It was basically totaled. All because an inexperienced driver had to prove that he could make it up the obstacle. Was it worth it? Had he had a spotter, had his lockers on and tires aired down properly, he probably would have made it without a giant repair bill. As it was, he had a huge towing bill, plus a repair bill of at least $10,000. I don't know about you, but I have better ways to spend my hard earned cash.

Off-road driving isn't just about hitting the gas and hoping for the best, it's an adventure that you create. Each type of off-road driving requires a different set of skills and approaches, making off-roading a diverse and exciting activity. Understanding these different types of off-road driving will unlock a treasure trove of adventure possibilities.

## The Main Types of Off-Roading

There are several different ways to enjoy Off-Road fun. Here are the main types of riding you will encounter.

**Rock Crawling**:

Rock crawling is an exhilarating form of off-road driving that requires the driver to take specialized vehicles over challenging obstacles. Rock crawling is all about pushing the limits of both the driver and vehicle.  Crawling usually requires modified 4WD vehicles to conquer incredibly challenging terrain.

**Overlanding**:

This is when people travel and live off the grid for a period of time. Sometimes for a week, sometimes for months. These adventurous individuals usually find scenic byways or off road trails in an effort to, as Robert Frost once wrote, to take "the road less traveled." It is an exciting and adventurous lifestyle for those who are cut out for it. In essence, Overlanding is boondocking on  steroids. It requires individuals to have self-sufficiency, navigation skills, and a love for exploring the great outdoors at your own pace.

**Dune Bashing or Dune Running**:

This type of off-roading requires drivers to take on the challenge of driving over the ever changing sand dunes (usually at pretty good speeds). In order to drive in the sand requires an ATV/OHV or 4-wheel drive vehicle that has

good clearance, deflated tires, and the power to dig through deep sand. Driving in sand dunes mixes the thrill of speed with the challenge of unpredictable terrain.

**Mudding:** It is exactly what it sounds like, mudding is riding through the mud. Of course, every child enjoys playing in the mud, but driving through mud in a proper off-road vehicle can be equally enjoyable. Because the Rocky Mountain states are normally fairly dry,  mudding isn't a normal thing to plan on out in the wild. So mudding often takes place on designated tracks that have been prepared for just such an event. Because of this, I will not be discussing mudding in this book. That is for another book at another time.

Each of the off-road styles discussed in this book has its own set of challenges and rewards. By understanding the nuances of each type, you can better prepare yourself for the adventures that lie ahead. It's not just about driving; it's about immersing yourself in nature, pushing your limits, and experiencing the thrill of off-road exploration.

## Buckle up and get ready

Assessing the level of difficulty of off-road trails is a crucial step in ensuring a successful and enjoyable off-road experience. If you know anything about Moab, Utah, then this scenario will make perfect sense. You are in your 4X4 and you're ready to tackle Moab's famous Hell's Revenge. You make it to the top and you are ready to take on the final obstacle, Hell's Gate. You are part way up the challenging V-shape run, when your enthusiasm starts to wane as your vehicle starts to slip and then tip, and you realize that you don't have lockers on your 4WD and no one to spot you, or pull you out. Trust me, that makes a good day turn bad real fast. To avoid such mishaps, it's essential to **evaluate** the trails based on your skills and your vehicle's capabilities.

So, how do you go about this off-road evaluation? You first need to take a moment to honestly assess your **off-road driving skills**. *Being self-aware* of your abilities behind the wheel sets the foundation for choosing the right trail. Remember, it's better to start easy and work your way up than to bite off more than you can chew…and end up at the bottom of a ravine or worse.

The next thing you need to consider is your **vehicle's capabilities**. Sure, your rig might look rough and ready, but is it really up for a challenging rock crawl or is it more suited for a scenic overlanding expedition? Matching your vehicle's strengths with the trail's demands ensures a smoother ride, both literally and figuratively. A stock SUV cannot handle the same rigors as a highly modified vehicle.

Once you've sized up your skills and your vehicle, it's time to consider the **trail's rating**. Just like movie ratings guide you on the intensity of the film, off-road trail ratings give you a heads-up on what to expect. From easy dirt roads to extreme rock challenges, these ratings provide a roadmap to help each driver find what trails are best for them. Trust these ratings just as you would a GPS on a long road trip. Trail ratings are created by experts and are usually quite accurate. If it shows the trail is an eight, and the roughest road you have ever driven is a four, you may want to reconsider that trail until you have a few more rides under your belt.

In the world of off-roading, wisdom lies in choosing the right path. No one wants to be the driver that bit off more than they could chew, and now you are stuck in a remote trail like a beached whale waiting for a very expensive recovery service to haul you and your broken ride back to the city.

Off-roading can be an exhilarating sport, but if you are not well-prepared it can be an expensive and dangerous activity. Ensuring a safe and enjoyable experience while navigating the trail's unique terrain goes beyond having a daring spirit; it's about embracing what I like to call, the Goldilocks principle: not too hard, not too easy, but just right for your skill level and vehicle's capabilities.

## The Terrain Tells No Tales

Here is a picture from my own personal experience on trail that I didn't know and had gone out alone. The road looked safe, but the shoulder was soft sand and completely slipped out from under me. Before I could try any countermeasure, I was already on my side.

Sizing up a trail for the first time is akin to speed dating; you need to make a quick and accurate assessment before diving in. It's essential to remember that the terrain isn't going to adapt for you; **it's immutable**. So it's up to you to make the adjustments needed before you take on the trail. Reading guidebooks, using online resources, and using the tried-and-true method of local knowledge are the best ways to determine if you need to make changes. Befriending a more experienced off-roader can be as valuable as finding a good sherpa before climbing Everest.

## Gear Up and Wise Up

Even the rosiest off-roading stories can come with thorns, and it all starts with gear selection. To make any off-road adventure end on a good note, you should equip your vehicle accordingly with the correct tires, recovery gear, and protection that suit the difficulty level of the trail you're about to take on. The right gear can be the difference between a successful excursion and a trip to a repair shop–or worse, the hospital.

## Know Your Limits

It is vital that you know both your limits and your vehicle's. For example, you wouldn't bring a poodle to a wolfpack showdown, so why take a city SUV to face a rock crawler's paradise? Being honest about your off-road driving skills isn't admitting defeat; it's plotting for future triumphs. Push your boundaries, but in a *controlled* fashion, Like adding Tabasco sauce to your taco, you don't pour the whole bottle on; you add one sprinkle at a time.

## Weather or Not

Reading the skies should become second nature to off-roaders; clouds are more than just beautiful white fluffy cotton balls in the sky. Weather can have a major impact on trail conditions; abrupt storms can transform parched riverbeds into raging flash flood torrents, or turn beautiful mountain trails into a greasy mess leading you down to sheer cliffs. A wise driver always checks and respects the weather forecast and knows when to postpone an adventure. It's better to be the one who walked away for another day on the mountain rather than the tragic story on the nightly news.

## Buddy System 2.0

Exploring solo can be a peaceful endeavor, but in off-roading, there's safety in numbers. It's not about forming a convoy, but having that reliable buddy who can pull you out of a jam— literally. Besides, shared misadventures make for the best campfire stories. Find fellow off-roaders with a similar skill level or enthusiasm for adventure and form alliances with them. When going on a trip to a new state or location that you have never been to, give a shout-out on Facebook or some other social media. It's amazing how many people will reach out that want to ride together.

If you do go out alone, always provide someone with your location via phone. There are several apps that will allow loved ones to track you if you don't return home when expected. IPhones have the Find My Phone app that allows you to track not only your phone, but people you care for. Android and IPhones can take advantage of Google's Find My Device. AirDroids also has

Apps such as Android Family Locator, which has so many features that it is like having a Swiss Army knife for your smartphone. Cerberus is another excellent app worth considering.

If you are ever going out alone, it is a wise rule of thumb to always let a friend or family member know where you are and when you expect to get back.

## Trail Etiquette

### Leave Only Tire Tracks

Off-roading comes with an unwritten pact to protect the playground that provides so much fun. It's simple: traverse with care, respect the flora and fauna, and take out what you bring in. Just like you wouldn't leave trash in a friend's car, don't do it to Mother Nature's domain. Driving responsibly ensures these trails remain open and pristine for future thrill-seekers. So *if you pack it in, always pack it out*.

Just as important as the pack-it-in/pack-it-out rule, is to never deface anything. It doesn't matter if a landowner has a sign that offends you, or if you think you are being funny by adding graffiti to some ancient wall art. It is wrong and can land you in jail. It also hurts future riding for the rest of us. There are several groups trying to close down our trails; by selfishly desecrating anything out in the wilderness you give them the ammo they need to shut trails down. So please, don't be that person!

## Hand Signals To Remember

Hand signals are an important way to communicate to each other on the road. It doesn't matter how well-marked the trails are; you still need to use hand signs to ride safely everywhere.

The correct hand signals are a quick and easy way to let riders coming the other way on the trail know how many people are in your group.

Always know where you are in line and how many people are behind you when you're going with a group. In a group of six, if someone comes up behind you, the lead driver will hold up five fingers to let them know that there are at least five people behind them. Each person does this based on where they are in line. You hold up a 5 if there are 5 or more riders behind you. For every rider after you, they should hold up the number of fingers to match the drivers still behind them. The last person in your group will put up their hand in a closed fist, which shows that there are no more riders coming in your party. If possible, it helps if the last driver also says, "There is no one behind me."

## Hand Signals to Use When Spotting

It's best to use hand signals along with voice commands since voice commands can be hard to hear at times. Also, you should use the words "driver" and "passenger" instead of "left" and "right," which can be hard for the driver and spotter to understand since they are often facing one another, so their lefts and rights will be opposite.

- Come Forward: To wave the driver in, put your hand or hands in the air with the palms facing you. Bring your palms toward your face as if to say come forward.
- Stop: A closed hand in a fist will tell the driver to stop.
- Turn: To turn the wheel, the driver should point with their index finger either to the left or right.
- To reverse or back up, open your hand facing the driver

and push backwards. This signal, along with moving the thumb to the index finger, tells the driver to back up a bit. Sometimes, the driver may need to move the vehicle to a better angle or back up and start the obstacle over again.

Before you start winching, you and your spotter should know a few hand signs that will help you stay safe.

- Winch In: A closed fist with both thumbs pointed in toward one another signals to winch in.

- Winch Out: A closed fist with thumbs pointed outward, away from one another, means to winch out.

- Stop: Closing the hand into a tight fist means to stop.

You may choose to use different hand gestures than those listed above, and that is fine as long as the driver and spotter agree and utilize the same hand signals. The ultimate goal is for you to be able to safely navigate your vehicle through challenging off-road hazards.

**Riding As A Group**

To keep the trails flowing smoothly, it is important to conduct all staging operations away from the trail and active obstacles, as well as to understand and follow the correct passing etiquette.

Slower-moving vehicles should keep to the right while faster-moving vehicles pass them on the left, similar to highway rules. By adhering to this advice, the flow of trail traffic is maintained, allowing individuals to drive at a speed that is most comfortable while ensuring safety at all times. When faster drivers are unable to overtake on the left due to limited space, it is the responsibility of the slower driver to maintain a steady flow of traffic. Slow drivers should be aware of vehicles behind them, and if they are impeding traffic, they should safely pull over, signal, and let faster-moving vehicles pass.

Avoid deviating off the trail to make way for others. Wait until you find a suitable area to allow someone to pass without driving on non-trail surfaces.

**Always let vehicles going uphill have the right-of-way**

Give the vehicle going uphill the right-of-way. You should always stop or back up to allow them to pass. When off-roading, vehicles that are going uphill need to keep their speed so as not to lose traction. Trust me, you will appreciate this rule when you are the one needing to have the right-of-way on a steep hill.

**Yield to hikers, mountain bikers, and horses**

Always give mountain bikers, hikers, and horses the right-of-way. These groups can't match your vehicle's power or speed. Slow down on paths to avoid dusting them and give them space. Also, take additional caution when approaching saddled horses. Stop on the side of the road and turn off your motor to prevent scaring them. And remember, they have as much right to be out enjoying the wilderness as you do.

**No Tailgating**

Trails are not for tailgating. When driving off-road, avoid getting too close to other drivers. If you get too close to the vehicle in front of you, a dust cloud can obscure your vision. When you can't see the rear differential on the vehicle ahead, you're too near. Give the vehicle in front of you extra room when ascending steep hills or negotiating difficult barriers. By keeping enough distance between you and the vehicle in front, you not only give them room to navigate, but you keep everyone safer.

Remember, if you are not moving as fast as those behind you, pull over and let them pass. This avoids tailgating, and makes for a safer trip for everyone concerned.

**Make Sure You Are Welcome**

True story–near where I live, an off-roader crossed onto some private property without permission and was met with a man holding a shotgun. Make sure that you don't enter property that is marked "keep out." It is wrong, and it could not only put you in danger, but by not obeying "No Trespassing" signs, it also hurts the entire off-roading community.

## Close the Gate Behind You

Also, on that note, some places don't mind off-roaders coming onto their property as long as you obey the rules. One major rule for all landowners is to always close any gate that you open. Having been raised on a cattle farm in Idaho, I know what a pain it is when your cattle get out. And if someone gets hurt because of an animal that got out and was hit by a car; well, that can bankrupt  whoever owned that animal. Never be the person who leaves a gate open.

## Slow Down, You Move To Fast

Yes, that was part of an old 1960s song, but when off-roading it can mean the difference between safety and serious injury.

## Stay On Marked Trails

Moab, Utah has been in the middle of a legal battle with the Federal Government to close several of their trails. One of the reasons this came about was because of the few off-roaders who refused to stay on the marked trails. Whenever we start creating our own trails, especially when it is on Federal or State land, those actions affect everyone who wants to continue riding and enjoying these great recreation areas. So please, always stay on marked trails.

## Avoid stopping in the middle of a trail

This protects you, and the driver coming up on a blind curve behind you, or around the bend in front of you. It is just common sense, but I have come upon more than one rider who nearly had my grill attached to their bumper—and I wasn't going very fast.

**Ready, Set, Off-road!**

**In the vast playground of off-road trails, there's a path waiting just for you.** With the knowledge gained from assessing different terrain types and difficulty levels, you're equipped to tackle the off-road world with confidence and precision. **So gear up, rev that engine, and let's hit the trails!**

# Chapter 2:

# Navigating with off-road Apps

As you get into the chapters that include the 100+ top trails, you will find that I recommend several apps to provide you with map information, directions, and/or coordinates for nearly every trail found in this book.

Some trails are truly hard to find if you don't have some guideposts along the way. These apps will provide guidance to help you both find your way to the trails, and back home again.

If you have done much off-roading at all, you will know that many trails are not well marked, and if you are like me, you have been lost more than once. These apps have saved my hide multiple times, and I don't ever go on a new trail without checking one or two of these apps to help get my bearings.

I personally have seven trail apps on my iPhone. I use five of these apps on a regular basis. I pay for the plus version on all of them, and it still costs me less than $130 per year. Considering how much money most of us spend on our hobby of off-roading, this is probably one of the smallest and yet most valuable investments you will ever make. If you don't believe me, spend one night lost out in the middle of nowhere, and you will become a true believer.

## Become a Digital Trailblazer

Let's face it, the ancient art of reading topographic maps and compasses is somewhat of a lost art in the age of smartphones. Once you learn how to use your apps properly,

your phone will become like a Swiss Army knife for your navigation. These apps help put the digital world at our fingertips, it's the smart off-roader who uses this power of technology to help enjoy the road less traveled.

## So, what's the best app?

In this book, I am not trying to crown a winner but rather to arm you with the knowledge to choose the one that best fits your personal needs. Each app has unique strengths that can help you travel less chartered roads more confidently. My goal is to help demystify these digital companions.

Choosing the best app or apps that are suited to your specific needs can help you navigate with the confidence of a well-seasoned driver.

Navigating through the great outdoors is "almost" always a thrilling adventure, and using these apps can help make your 4-wheeling experience even more enjoyable. These handy tools bring a whole new level of help for your off-road expeditions. Many of these apps offer features like **trail mapping**, **offline accessibility**, and **waypoint marking**. They provide you with the ability to explore remote trails without worrying about losing a signal or missing a turn. That's the power these navigation apps can help bring to your outdoor adventure.

**Trail mapping** is an essential feature of off-road apps. It allows you to discover new trails and how to plan your routes much more effectively. With these detailed trail maps, you can explore with the confidence of knowing exactly where you are and where you're headed, and just as importantly, how to get back to the trailhead. Several of these apps provide virtual maps that can help guide you along your route, ensuring a smooth and enjoyable experience.

**Offline accessibility** has become a real game-changer for any off-road enthusiast who plans to venture into areas with limited or no cellphone signal. Imagine yourself in the middle of a remote area, surrounded by imposing mountains or thick forests, and discovering that your phone has no signal. If it hasn't happened to you yet–it will. *Cue the panic!* It is important to determine which of these navigational apps provide offline accessibility so that you can download maps beforehand and access them even when you're off the grid. It's like having a portable GPS that works anywhere, anytime.

**Waypoint marking**. This feature allows you to bookmark specific locations along your route. Waypoints allow you to review pictures that others have taken. This can help you avoid getting lost. It also allows you to use your phone to take pictures to document your journey; whether it's a breathtaking overlook, or a section of the trail that is extra tricky and may require extra clearance or special equipment such as a winch. These waypoints can help you navigate back to the trailhead (think of it as leaving a digital trail of breadcrumbs) while providing digital help for future travelers.

In a world where technology continues to shape our outdoor experiences, off-road navigation apps have become indispensable tools for anyone who wants to venture off-road.

## The World of Off-Road Navigation Apps

When it comes to choosing the right off-road app for you, it's crucial to understand the strengths and weaknesses of the different options available to you. There are over a dozen different apps out there that you can use. Some are free, and others have a fee. I have tried several with varying success.

In this book, I will reference the apps that I use most. You may have others that you prefer, but I have found the following to work best for me personally. The apps I will reference in the book as trail sources are the following: OnX off-road, Alltrails, Avenza Maps, Gaia GPS, Trails Offroad, Trailforks, Backcountry Navigator GPS Pro, and Overland Bound One.

There are other apps that work better outside the USA, but I cannot speak to how well they work, so you will have to experiment to find which will work best for you in foreign countries.

**OnX Off-Road**

This app stands out for its comprehensive trail mapping for off-roading, because it is specifically made for people who want to go off the beaten path. (**OnXmaps** included in both premium & elite package) and offline accessibility, making it a reliable companion when venturing into remote areas. I find this app very useful since it was made specifically for people who go 4-wheeling.

The Pros to OnX Off-road

- It finds trails for SxS, 4x4, ATV, dirt bike, and snowmobiles nationwide. Tap any trail for open/close dates, difficulty ratings, and images. See 500K campgrounds, trailheads, and boat launches.

- Save Maps to use offline. You can save interactive land and trail maps on your phone or tablet. The integrated GPS on your phone will let you see your location on saved maps.

- Track, Save, Share Trips. The GPS lets Go & Track track your location, distance, elevation, and more.

- Markup Customization. It allows you to map your route. Mark campsites, vehicle parking, and trail intersections with Waypoints.

**Sync with CarPlay and Android Auto**

- It provides up-to-date trail information and detailed maps even when you're off the grid, helping ensure that you never lose your way.

- It makes it easy to create and share notes in the app.

The cons to OnX Off-road

- Some users may find the interface slightly complex, especially if you are new to off-road navigation apps.
- It has been reported by some that it can have some glitchy functionality with Apple Carplay. I personally have not had that issue.
- The free version is very limited in what it offers.
- It can be laggy when you use it with other apps in the background.

The OnX company provides both premium and elite versions. For the money, I personally find the premium version does just fine for most users' needs–unless you are looking for bargains on off-road supplies. The big plus to the elite version is the discounts it provides swag, supplies and equipment. So if you are buying a lot of off-road supplies, the additional cost for the elite version may well save you hundreds, if not thousands down the road. For example, if you save 20% on a new Warn winch, that extra few bucks for the elite version more than paid for itself.

**Alltrails**

This is a very good option for off-road enthusiasts who appreciate having access to a vast database of trails. Alltrails+ has a strong community-driven approach. This app offers a plethora of user-generated content, helping you discover new trails based on real experiences. It is one of the best hiking apps on the market, but is more limited when it comes to off-roading trails. Users can add their own new trails and save favorite trails to customizable lists. It is a great app to help find your way home via digital breadcrumbs to backtrack if you get lost.

This app provides both a free version and a pro version, branded as **Alltrails+**. Many people find the free version very helpful, but I personally believe that the additional benefits that come with the Plus version are worth the money.

Pros of the AllTrails+ app:

The desktop platform and app for AllTrails have a contemporary appearance. Finding trails based on location, activity, and slope level is simple. Additional benefits include of:

- a database with more than 400,000 trail routes worldwide.

- the ability to look for trails in your current location or on your intended route.

- Many search filters to help you choose a route that fits your goals, experience, and level of fitness.

- Reviews and information provided by a group of outdoor enthusiasts.

Cons to the AllTrails app:

- Paying Pro members are the only ones who have access to offline maps.

- You need to have mobile phone reception in order to utilize the maps in the app if you have a free subscription.

- Practical completion instructions for the route are not well-defined.

- You'll need to look elsewhere for more information if you're looking for anything more than a brief rundown of the trip.

**Trails Offroad**

Trails Offroad is another app developed for off-road enthusiasts. It appeals to those seeking curated trail guides and reliable navigation assistance. With a focus on quality over quantity, this app offers handpicked trail recommendations and detailed descriptions, ensuring a satisfying experience. It allows you to download and use your maps offline. It also has a feature that I love called "follow mode" which provides waypoints with pictures to help make sure you are going where you intended to travel.  It also provides a scroll around the map to see local trails and potential routes, even in offline mode. The trails are always color-coded based on the trail's difficulty.

Pros to Trails Offroad

- Its user trail reviews are useful for trip planning.
- You can learn from shared experiences. For instance, blocked or open trails, melted snow, etc.
- Directions to the trailhead and end.
- Download GPX files for Gaia GPS and other programs.
- Trails are printable.
- It is easy to use.

Cons to Trails offroad

- Its trail database may be narrower compared to other apps with larger user bases.
- For people outside of the US, there are fewer trails available.
- You can not rely on it as your only option. This is because, while useful for planning and trail discovery, it is not always suitable for navigation.

 It has a free membership, but to get the true value of this app, you really need to pay for the annual all-access membership.

**Avenza Maps**

This app shines in its user-friendly interface and extensive map library, ideal for those who prioritize ease of use. By providing access to a wide range of maps, including topographic and satellite imagery, Avenza Maps ensures you have the necessary tools for a successful journey.

You can buy or download maps from the in-app Map Store.

Their Plus subscription allows for an infinite number of imports of custom maps. Avenza Maps operates through a yearly subscription model.

Pros of Avenza Maps:

- Free to use (no subscription required to access up to three maps at once)
- Usability: Avenza is really simple for a beginner to learn and use.
- A large number of usable maps: You can use any georeferenced PDF.
- Incredibly efficient and obtains the finest GPS signal from your device
- It almost never crashes.
- Simple data export for use with Google Maps or other free applications
- As long as two or more maps share common areas, layers can be seen simultaneously on those maps.
- Possesses excellent measurement tools: Azimuth collection is one that the collector lacks.

Cons of Avenza Maps:

- Lack of synchrony Data is solely local, and exporting it is the only method to access it.
- The PDF map's level of detail is limited. The degree of detail depends on how detailed the PDF is. You are able to obtain significantly more detail on the basis feature you are utilizing because collector uses vector data.
- There are no means to share dashboards and real-time dynamic data with your clients or team.

**Gaia GPS**

This app is very good if detailed topographic maps are your top priority.    This app delivers exceptional accuracy and customization options. Whether you're tracking elevation changes or planning precise routes, this app caters to off-road enthusiasts who prefer in-depth mapping features.

There is a free version of this app; however, the free version is very limited and cannot be used offline. To get the full potential of their mapping service, you need to pay for the premium version.

Pros of Gaia GPS

- Premium topographic maps for off-grid travels
- Excellent offline access
- Several map layers and overlays
- Strong track record
- Versatile and customizable.

Cons of Gaia GPS

- The main con to Gaia GPS is the learning curve for new users, and may require patience to fully harness its capabilities.
- It has very limited social features.
- Syncing requires good internet.
- Few customer service alternatives.

This app was originally developed for hikers and backpackers and is really much stronger as a hiker's app, but I have used it for certain off-roading trails as well.

**Backcountry Navigator GPS Pro**

This is a navigation tool that is both versatile and customizable, making it an ideal choice for anyone in the backcountry. It is important to remember when looking at this app that it was developed mainly for hikers, and that is the audience it mainly caters too. Nevertheless, this app appeals to users who like customizing their navigation experience because it offers a number of sophisticated features like route planning and waypoint marking.

Pros to Backcountry Navigator GPS Pro

- It works well as a navigation app for Android phones and tablets.

- It lets you use the GPS on your Android device to navigate and save a variety of maps for offline use.

- It works great with Android Wear, allowing you to see your navigation on your wrist.

- You can use GPS waypoints from both GPX or KML files.

- It uses several free publicly available map sources that you can download.

Cons to Backcountry Navigator GPS Pro

- It is new to iPhones, so it does not work as well as other apps when using Apple products.

- Its abundance of options may overwhelm beginners seeking a more straightforward solution.

It has three tiers of membership that users can choose from depending on their specific needs.

**Trailforks**

Trailforks is mainly known as an app designed for mountain bikers and gravel cyclists. However, I have found that it can be very handy. Trailforks provides interactive trail maps, a topographic layer, points of interest, trail popularity (again more for bikers), heatmaps, routes, trail conditions, photos, videos and more. This app has over 15,000 trails worldwide for off-roading.

The pros to this app are:

- For desktop use, it is free. The Pro version requires a monthly or annual subscription.
- The website has trail maps for every location on the planet.
- Routes and recommendations for modifications to the trail maps are welcome from users.
- Data is accessible in an offline manner.
- Every region's trail maps are available for download.
- It does have the ability to designate between trails that are wide enough for ATV's, SXS, and regular SUVs/Jeeps.

The cons to this app are:

- Because TrailForks is heavily weighted towards mountain bikes, trail runners and hikers may find it challenging to find a lot of routes.
- Some users report that the app periodically crashes and takes a long time to load.
- It is necessary to download every trail region separately.
- To access maps offline, you must purchase the Pro edition.

**Overland Bound One**

Lastly, Overland Bound One caters mainly to the overlanding community, offering a blend of navigation tools and social networking features. This app is ideal for connecting with like-minded off-road enthusiasts and sharing experiences, fostering a sense of community on your off-road journeys.

Pros to Overland Bound One:

- Members get access to offline mapping and GPS navigation, community support, offroad trails, trip planning, upcoming events, and more.

- They also suggest places to camp, places to restock on fuel and water, local mechanics, and the ability to message other members that may be in their vicinity.

Cons to Overland Bound One:

- Its focus on overlanding may limit its appeal to users primarily interested in trail mapping and navigation.
- It is great for overlanding, but not as much for other types of off-road adventurers.

As with any of these apps, I believe you really need to decide if they provide everything you want before you pay the membership fee.

There are other apps, like "The Dryt," are excellent for campers but do not address the wants and needs of off-road enthusiasts. For that reason, I will not get into any of those types of apps in this book.

I also have Wikiloc which is a very good app. It is mainly used for hikers, but it does an Off-Road filter. I personally think that Wikiloc is better suited for trails listed overseas. When I travel overseas, this is a great app; but some of the other trail apps work better for me in the US.

Understanding the strengths and weaknesses of these popular off-road navigation apps is key to selecting the one(s) that best aligns with your navigation needs. Each app offers unique features and benefits, so consider your priorities and preferences to make an informed choice that enhances your off-road experiences.

But after all this, what app to choose? I have found that talking to other off-roading enthusiast is a great way to learn which one(s) are right for you. I personally use several of these apps depending on specific needs of where I am planning to go. But whatever you choose, always consider signal strength, or the lack thereof. Off-road apps should know how to play solo; offline accessibility is like having a reliable buddy who sticks around when the party—aka cell service—is gone. Make sure the app you choose doesn't ghost you when you meander into the boonies. I always love an app the can provide digital trail breadcrumbs; when you are lost (and trust me, you will be at some point) those digital breadcrumbs that can help you backtrack out the way you came in can save you a cold night alone in the wilderness.

If you are just starting out, I strongly recommend you consider **ease of use** when picking an app. Trust me from personal experience, you don't want to be fumbling with an app while maneuvering through a tricky washout or dangerous mountain ledge. If you relate to this more than you'd like to admit, you should favor an app with an interface so simple that even your technophobe uncle could navigate it.

When the rubber meets the road, it's about marrying your needs to the app's strengths. Be picky, be choosy—after all, you wouldn't take a sports car rock crawling. Look through the list, watch some YouTube videos about each one, then test drive a few, and settle on the navigator app or apps that not only helps find your way to and from your journey, but also aligns with your off-road spirit, and technical abilities. Then grab your phone or tablet, kiss indecision goodbye, and let the right app(s) be the compass to your off-road adventures.

If you find any of the apps confusing, they all have videos on YouTube that explain how they work, and how to best use all their bells and whistles.

**One last note** to finish this chapter. After all is said and done, don't completely ditch your boy-scout compass and old fashioned folding paper maps, sometimes they are still the best solution.

# Chapter 3:
# Tools Of The Trade

## Pimp Your Ride: The Off-Roader's Checklist

The relentless riddle of the trails demands that your rig be ready for anything you want to throw at it. And unless you have a very rich uncle that can take some stress off of your pocket book, it can be financially challenging. I don't know who coined this saying, but it has plenty of truth mixed in with the humor, "Off-roading is the art of getting dirty and going broke while slowly going nowhere and taking all day to get there."

The truth is that tires, suspension, engine, and brakes, all need to be in better harmony than the Beatles in order to create the perfect ride. But it's important to remember that you aren't auditioning your vehicle for "Pimp My Ride," but rather an off-road edition of "Survivor." So, unless you have a bottomless pocketbook, you should ditch the ego and **upgrade where needed**. The most important places to start gearing up are gnarly all-terrain tires and a suspension that won't buckle when the going gets tough. Your vehicle needs to have armour stronger than that of a crusader knight, to defend your underbelly with skid plates so that you are protected from rocks poking giant holes in your oil pan or other area that can be damaged. From personal experience, having a skid plate may cost you some cash up front, but the first time you have a giant granite boulder trying to rip into your oil pan, you will thank the day you got a skid plate. If you are just looking to invest in an off-road vehicle, make sure that the vehicle you are investing in has sufficient under armor. Most serious off-road vehicles come from the factory with strong skid plates attached.

**Roll out with recovery essentials**. Think of your winch and recovery straps as your off-road BFFs. They're there to pull you out of any hole you will get yourself into, while a high-lift jack (aka farmer's jack), recovery traction boards, and a shovel are like the Swiss army knives for any off-road challenges. Those few items will give you extra peace of mind as you roll off the pavement.

When it comes to navigating Mother Nature's labyrinth, the **right tools are half the battle**. The roll bar isn't just for show, it can literally save your a...behind. A first aid kit should be your constant companion, and a smartphone or GPS is your digital map to guide you both to the fun and back home again.

## Suspension: The Great Equalizer

An experienced off-road mechanic could write entire chapters on suspension alone, but for this book, I will keep it brief. Needless to say, when it comes to off-roading, your vehicle's suspension system is like a workhorse silently toiling away to ensure your ride doesn't turn into a chiropractor's nightmare. Wait, perhaps that's not entirely silent, as anyone who's had their teeth rattled out of their mouth on a rugged trail can testify.

There's a variety of suspension systems out there - namely these three. You can choose from the **independent front suspension**, offering a smoother ride on less challenging terrains, to the **solid front axle**, which gives you that 'conquer anything' feel, to the **long-travel suspension** that essentially lets you handle boulders with ease. Think of it as a dance between your vehicle and the terrain, where the suspension leads, and control and stability follow. Without the proper suspension setup, you're not so much dancing as you are in stomping competition; which can be both ungraceful and uncomfortable. Having driven in vehicles with and without the proper suspension, I can say from personal experience, your suspension makes a world of difference.

## Traction: The Unsung Hero of Grip

Ever seen a mountain goat effortlessly scaling a steep cliff? That's your off-road vehicle with the right traction system. Proper all-terrain tires, differentials, lockers, and traction control systems work in concert to ensure your vehicle maintains a solid embrace with the ground beneath it, no matter how uncooperative the terrain might be. These systems are the difference between powering through a muddy slope with the grace of a drunken elephant, or gripping the track with the tenacity of a cougar hunting it's prey. Mastery of your traction system means you'll spend less time inventing new curse words and more time enjoying the scenery.

## Airing Down

Tire pressure management, more precisely the process of "airing down," is one of the most important components of off-roading, although it is sometimes overlooked by novices. Experienced enthusiasts, on the other hand, hold this feature in the highest regard.

When off-roading, proper tire pressure is essential. It can have a big impact on the safety the operation of your vehicle in rocky or sandy conditions. In essence, you increase the tire's surface area in touch with the ground by decreasing the tire pressure when you air down your tires. This simple but effective method maximizes the off-roading experience by improving traction and facilitating easier handling over uneven terrain.

To "air down," or lower the tire pressure, we mean to a level that is much lower than what you'd use for normal driving on the road. Off-roaders often do this because it lets the tires spread out and make a bigger, more aggressive track. Airing down the tire results in better speed and better grip on difficult surfaces like sand, mud, rocks, and gravel.

There are four main benefits to airing down your tires before going off-road.

- Improved Traction
  - Airing down increases the amount of contact your tires will have with the ground. The more rubber that is in contact with the road, the better the traction. Driving over loose surfaces like sand, mud, or gravel requires this. More traction means more control, making difficult terrain and steep inclines easier.
- Improved Ride Comfort
  - Airing down tires can greatly reduce bumpiness of the trail, giving you and your passengers a more comfortable ride. Lower air pressure helps tires absorb shock from rocks, potholes, and other impediments.
- Lower Puncture Risk
  - When deflated properly, tires can better conform to sharp things and avoid punctures. This flexibility lowers tire damage, letting you more confidently navigate tough terrain.

The performance of your off-road vehicle and the longevity of your tires both depend on knowing how much air to put into your tires. Here are some basic recommended guidelines for tire pressure during various off-road conditions.

- Sand or Loose Gravel: Use 12-15 psi to improve your tire's footprint and help prevent your vehicle from sinking.

- Rocky terrain: 15-20 psi helps tires wrap around boulders and avoid punctures.

- Mud: 15-20 psi can prevent sticking, depending on depth and stickiness.

- Snow: Like sand, 12-15 psi helps your vehicle 'float' on snow.

When buying new tires, talk to the dealer and ask what recommendations the factory has provided for different off-road conditions.

The following important variables may affect how much you should air down:

- Tire Construction: Compared to bias-ply tires, radial tires may typically be aired down much more.

- Vehicle Weight: Lower pressures may be needed for heavier vehicles than for lightweight ones.

- Rim Size: To keep the tire from coming off the rim, vehicles with larger rims should run with a little more air in the tires than those running on smaller rim to tire ratio.

- Driving Speed: To avoid an excessive build-up of heat, tires must be inflated to a greater pressure at higher driving speeds.

Airing down too much can cause issues. Too much deflation can unseat tires from rims, especially during aggressive cornering or quick driving. Sharp pebbles and other impediments can damage tires with extremely low pressure. Finally, returning to pavement and driving at higher speeds without re-inflating your tires may cause poor handling and tire damage.

**After off-roading, always re-inflate your tires immediately before returning to highway use.** Driving with deflated tires on the highway can ruin the tires, and make your vehicle harder to navigate at higher speeds.  To prolong the life of your tires, it is advised to reinflate them even if you are storing your off-highway vehicle on a trailer.

## Recovery Gear: The Emergency Kit You Can't Overlook

Imagine setting off on a trail and meeting the Mud Pit from Hell. But fear not—you've brought your recovery gear, haven't you? A strong **kinetic snatch rope**, a good **soft shackle with a recovery ring**, **traction boards**, a **hi-lift jack**, and a **winch** are the essentials of off-road rescue. They are essential in getting you out of sticky, or should I say, slippery situations. Investing in these tools and knowing how to use them means that you can brave even treacherous terrains with confidence. Plus, you'll be the trail's MVP when you inevitably need to rescue that overconfident new guy who brought their street car to the  'all-terrain' party.

## Armor and Protection: Your Off-Road Suit of Armor

Now, even if you fancy yourself as a modern-day road knight, your off-road vehicle needs its protection. Skid plates, rock sliders, and roll cages might not sound as cool as 'chain mail,' but they are just as important. They are there to take the hits so that the rest of your vehicle doesn't have to.  Your battles with rogue tree stumps and aggressive boulders may help make your tales of glory sound better; and with the proper protection, it can be done without expensive repair bills.  These steel guardians make sure the only scars you come back with are the brag-worthy ones, and not the ones that make your wallet weep.

## Communication and Navigation: Don't Get Lost, Talk About It

The backcountry is not the place to test your 'inner compass'-- even though I have tried and failed. Solid communication and navigation systems should never be considered optional accessories. GPS devices and good old fashioned maps can ensure your route is clear and that you return triumphant rather than spending a cold night out alone on the mountain.

Also, if you spend a lot of time in areas where you do not have any cell service, and you are not with a group of riders, you should really consider owning a satellite communicator (good ones are available for under $300). These little units can literally mean the difference between life and death if you get in serious trouble out in the mountains or desert.

In our research, here are a few good satellite communication options we think are worth considering:

- The Best On-Device Communicator is the SPOT X
- The Best Budget Satellite Messenger is the ZOLEO Satellite Messenger
- Budget Satellite Overall Messenger we found is the Bivy Stick
- Best Overall Satellite Messenger we found is the Garmin inReach Messenger
- The Most Feature-Rich Satellite Messenger is the Garmin inReach Mini 2
- Best GPS Device Satellite Messenger is the Garmin GPSMAP 67i

Staying within your comfort zone while off-roading might not initially sound that adventurous, but in the long run it is the best option. By understanding and respecting the framework composed of suspension, traction, recovery gear, armor, and communication and navigation systems, you give yourself the foundation to stretch those comfort zones safely. As time and experience grow, your skills combined with the vehicle's capabilities will allow you continue your exploration of more challenging terrains. By doing so, the off-road experience remains exciting yet controlled; thus striking that delicate balance of have a great experience with some good stories to tell, without becoming a cautionary tale to the next driver as you lay in the hospital–or worse.

Now that we have all the important items out of the way, let's dive into the fun part. Finding rides across the Rocky Mountains that will expand your off-road repertoire of fun.

**If you ask ten people which are the best off-roading trails found in each of these states in order, you will most likely get ten differing answers.** This list was put together by reviewing several off-road websites, talking with local experts, gathering information from state recreation's representatives, local BLM offices, and from my personal adventures–and misadventures. I also tried to give a good cross-section that includes easy trails for beginners, and kick-ass trails for those of you who love the challenge of making it up the type of trail that will make a less adventurous person's hair turn gray. So,

I understand that some of you will disagree with the trail choices in this book. That being said, don't shoot me if you disagree with the choices herein. As Elton John said, "I'm just the piano player."

Note that most of the trails listed in this book do not have any fees associated with riding. Those that do charge fees are mentioned in their descriptions.

# Chapter 4:

# Finding the Best Trails and Trail Systems in Arizona

If you don't remember the previous page, here is a recap for anyone who wasn't paying attention. My list is not to be considered the consummate order, but these trails are consistently rated as the ten best trails. That being said, all of these trails will give you a guaranteed fun ride that I can guarantee you won't soon forget.

## Arizona OHV Permit Rules

In order to operate on public and state trust lands in Arizona, both resident and non-resident off-highway vehicles (OHVs) that weigh 2,500 pounds or less and were intended by the manufacturer primarily for use over  unimproved terrain are required by law to display a valid OHV decal. Jeeps, SUVs, pickup trucks, and other recreational vehicles are not obliged to obtain an OHV decal.

## Get Ready For Fun

There are thousands of miles of trails, roads, and open spaces in Arizona that are suited for off-highway vehicles (OHVs), motorcycles, and all-terrain vehicles (ATVs). If you want to get away from the crowds and experience off-roading, Arizona is the place to go. Among the enormous open spaces that Arizona has to offer are views of red-rock buttes, deserts that are covered with cacti, and magnificent alpine forests.

If you love riding through the great outdoors, Arizona extends a warm welcome. So without further adieu, let's jump right in...

## Broken Arrow Trail – Sedona, AZ

Trail Rating: Moderately difficult between 6-7

Trail Type: out and back

Trail Length: 3.7 miles

Approximate Time: 2 - 3 hours

Best Season: Spring through Fall

Traffic: Busy (tours and off-road groups frequent this trail)

Trailhead Coordinates: 111°45'24.7"W and 34°50'44.0"N

Broken Arrow is the pinnacle of off-road trails in Sedona, with challenging slick rock obstacles set against the majestic red walls of the landscape. Some people claim that this trail provides the most stunning scenery in Sedona, attracting a variety of outdoor enthusiasts such as hikers, mountain bikers, and you guessed it, off-roaders.

If you want one of the most fun rodeo rides your 4X4 can provide, keep your eyes peeled and hands on the steering wheel, and you'll have a blast on one of Arizona's top off-road trails.

Heart-pounding ascents, descents, and cross-axle ditches can all be experienced on this trail quite safely, thanks to the trail's easy-to-follow markings. That being said, driving in a distracted or reckless manner can lead to some less-than-pleasant outcomes in the midst of the steep cliffs and deep crevices continually sprinkled along this trail.

The biggest challenge on this trail is the infamous Devil's Staircase. This set of shelves demand a decent amount of space underneath and is filled with rocks and holes that make it even more challenging. It's safest to stick to the familiar route taken by the Sedona Pink Jeep tours (yes, it should be obvious to you), but be cautious because once you're on the Staircase, you may find yourself gradually losing control, even with the brakes fully engaged. So, take your time and only proceed down this obstacle in line with the other vehicles. Lastly, the trail's entrance is in a residential neighborhood, so make sure to keep the noise down to a dull purr. Also, there is limited parking space, so it is inadvisable for unlicensed vehicles to park trailers there.

This trail is extremely well-liked among off-roading groups and tour companies, so be ready to yield to Pink Jeeps whenever possible, they know the trail and can safely move at a quicker pace than you.

You can view GPS trail maps, conditions, difficulty, and more on any of these three reliable apps: OnX Offroads, or AllTrails+, or TrailsOffroad.

## Crown King Trail (Backway to Crown King) – Crown King, AZ

Trail Rating: Difficult 7.5

Trail Type: 1-way or out and back

Trail Length: 27.3 miles

Approximate Time: 3-6 hours

Best Season: Spring through Fall

Traffic: Busy

Trailhead Coordinates: 33.9506634, -112.3132616

This demanding off-road trail in Prescott National Forest provides an excellent chance for historical exploration.

Although the majority of the route is manageable, there are some challenging sections that will test standard stock 4X4 vehicles. The most challenging section in the final four miles has worsened over time, revealing additional rocks and deep ruts. Assertive off-road vehicles with strong articulation can still conquer this trail, although they might require assistance from a tow strap.

This trail is quite lengthy at twenty-seven miles and presents a good challenge for those that are up to it. It is definitely not a trail for a newbie unless they are traveling with more experienced drivers.. Although there are ways around the tougher challenges, this path is still no walk in the park. It is essential to have a high-clearance vehicle equipped with 4-wheel drive. Lockers and other adjustments will be beneficial. This trail is considered a moderate difficulty level, but the conditions can vary based on recent storms and maintenance. During peak season, the trail is bustling with activity, being one of Arizona's most frequented routes, always attracting a large number of visitors. Watch out for blind spots and be aware of traffic approaching from behind. Be prepared for a significant number of Jeeps and riders if you choose to tackle this trail over the weekend. This day trip is a blast, allowing you to put your vehicle to the test while discovering the beauty of the southern Bradshaw Mountains. The trail is accessible all year long, however winter may pose some additional challenges, but it is a stunning destination no matter when you go.

You can view GPS trail maps, conditions, and difficulty and more on any of these apps; OnX Offroads, or AllTrails+, or TrailsOffroad.

## Arizona Peace Trail - Quartzsite, AZ

Trail Rating: Moderate 4.5

Trail Type: end-to-end or giant loop

Trail Length: 675+ miles for the entire loop trail, short segments of varying lengths

Approximate Time: 5 hours up to 4 days

Best Season: Year-Round but best time to visit is from mid-September through March

Traffic: Low to Moderate (some sections are traveled more than others)

Trailhead Coordinates: 33.6807° N, 114.2081° W

The Arizona Peace Trail is an Overlander's wet dream—paradise in the desert. The entire trail is nearly seven hundred miles of wilderness, and it takes several days to traverse.

The entire Peace Trail is made up of 32 segments that can be taken as varying lengths of day trips for those who do not want the entire overland experience. The trail also has additional roads and trails that include almost 1,000 miles of additional outdoor fun. You can drive the trail all year long. Most any stock 4x4 should be able handle the entire route without any issues. The great thing about the Peace Trail is that it can literally provide weeks of off-road fun for those who want to do the entire trail and all it's subsidiary trails along the way.

Here are two short segments that are traveling should you not want to run the entire distance.

## Peace Trail West

Trailhead Coordinates: 33.58303, -114.37675

Located close to Quartzsite, Arizona, this point-to-point track spans a distance of 92 miles. It is generally considered to be a path that is moderately tough. It is highly unlikely that you will come across many other people while you are exploring this track.

To learn more about this portion of the trail, check out the mapping directions found on the AllTrails+ app, with maps also found on the Avenza app. There are also two great websites the provide a plethora of information about the Peace Trail; they are the Arizona Peace Trail website or Quartzsiteoffroad.com.

## The Salome to Harquahala Peak Spur

Trailhead Coordinates: 33.94613, -113.66939

This track is about 8 miles long and has a lot of loose and steep climbs and is somewhat narrow. ATVs, UTVs, and dirt bikes are more appropriate on the section of this path that lies south of Salome Road. North of Salome Road, you will find scenic trails that work much better for standard sizes 4X4s. There is one wash  crossing that needs to be passed with more clearance.

This spur runs off from the main peace trail (not from any main road). Find out more about this part of the trail by following the directions on the OnX Offroad app to the Salome to Harquahala Peak spur.

# Box Canyon Off-Road – Florence Junction, AZ

Trail Rating: Moderate 5

Trail Type: Out and Back

Trail Length: 18 miles each way

Approximate Time: 3-4 hours

Best Season: Fall to Spring

Traffic: Heavy

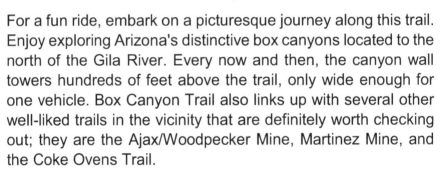

Trailhead Coordinates: 33.10386, -111.26525

For a fun ride, embark on a picturesque journey along this trail. Enjoy exploring Arizona's distinctive box canyons located to the north of the Gila River. Every now and then, the canyon wall towers hundreds of feet above the trail, only wide enough for one vehicle. Box Canyon Trail also links up with several other well-liked trails in the vicinity that are definitely worth checking out; they are the Ajax/Woodpecker Mine, Martinez Mine, and the Coke Ovens Trail.

To explore this stunning trail and its amazing box canyons, you will coordinate out of Florence, Arizona The simplest path starts at Price Road. For those looking for an adventure off the beaten path, we suggest taking Mineral Mountain Road. This picturesque trail provides a challenging terrain, ideal for off-road fans and thrill-seekers seeking an exciting experience. Down in the canyon, you'll face some tough hurdles. Price Road is a great option for new drivers or anyone looking for a relaxed and easy drive. Take in the stunning natural beauty around you while you savor a peaceful and scenic drive through the canyon. For those who love adventure and seek a more difficult journey, Mineral Mountain Road is the perfect destination. Grab your hat and get ready for challenging terrain, tricky sections, and thrilling moments that will put your skills to the test and push you to your limits, bringing an extra level of excitement to your canyon journey. The great part is that you can choose between the laid-back path from Price Road or the challenging appeal of Mineral Mountain Road, the canyon offers breathtaking scenery and a memorable off-road adventure.

Along different parts of the trail you will find several large rounded boulders that need precise tire positioning. Stock SUVs with strong ground clearance can handle it. Be sure and check the weather forecast in the area, and avoid going into the canyon during a heavy rainstorm as there are potentially dangerous flash floods.

This trail has received the honor of being on the Most Dangerous Roads blog. You can also get maps, status reports, waypoints, and more on either the AllTrails+, Trails Offroad, and OnX Offroads apps.

## Schnebly Hill Road - Sedona, AZ

Trail Rating: Moderately Easy 3

Trail Type: Out and Back

Trail Length: 11 miles each way

Approximate Time: 2 hours

Best Season: Spring-Fall, closed Winters

Traffic: Heavy

Trailhead Coordinates: 34.866431, -111.748648

With a view that is unquestionably one of the finest in Sedona, this road drops more than 2,200 feet from the top of the massive Mogollon Rim down into Sedona, making it one of Arizona's most scenic routes. It presents majestic red rock buttes set against a lush forest and a vivid blue sky. Various unforgettable hiking trails start from different locations along the road, and camping is permitted above Vista Point. Elk or deer may make an appearance before the sun goes down, and those seeking a leisurely end-of-day drive will appreciate the ride downhill.

The signs recommend using specialized high-clearance 4X4s or street-legal OHVS, however some higher-clearance cars, like the Subaru Outback Wilderness may be able to navigate the terrain. The road is spacious and in good condition but be prepared for some bumps along the way. A significant part of the lower section consists of a shelf road.

The Dangerous Roads Blog calls Schnebly Hill Road an amusement ride. You can also get GPS maps, waypoints, trail updates, and more on any of these apps; AllTrails, OnXRoads, and Trails Offroad.

## Hot Wells Dunes Recreation Area – Safford, AZ

Trail Rating: From Easy 2 to Moderately Hard 7

Trail Type: OHV recreation area

Trail Length: 2,000 acres of sand dunes

Approximate Time:  Varies

Best Season: October-March, Open year-round

Traffic: Varies

Trailhead Coordinates: 32.523693 -109.426624

Hot Well Dunes Recreation Area is a dune-basher's paradise. It is perfect for off-highway vehicle (OHV) enthusiasts, providing 2,000 acres of rolling dunes to discover. Formed ages ago by natural forces, this region offers gentle dunes for casual OHV riders and steep hills for those craving an adrenaline rush.

But there's more to it than just off-roading. At Hot Well Dunes' campground, solar power heats up water from an artesian well, filling two tubs for visitors to relax and rejuvenate after a day in the dunes.

Due to its desert location, Hot Well Dunes experiences summer temperatures of around 100+ degrees Fahrenheit, which can make camping and outdoor activities uncomfortable from June to September. For the best weather, consider visiting during the fall or spring seasons. To steer clear of the masses, who tend to flock in large numbers on weekends—especially during Easter weekend, opt for a visit on a weekday.

Directions to trailhead: Take Highway 70 for seven miles east from Safford. Take Haekel Road (BLM) to the right (south), and drive 15 ½ miles to the location. Fan Road: Take Central Avenue two miles north from Bowie to reach Fan Road. Proceed one mile east on Fan and then one mile north on Donahue. To get to Haekel, turn east on Rosewood and travel six kilometers along it. To get there, drive nine more miles north. Tanque Road: Highway 191 offers access to this road. Milepost 105 is not far from the Tanque Road turnoff on Highway 191. Hot Well Dunes Recreation Area charges $3 per vehicle each day, whether you camp, relax in the tubs, or ride the dunes.

You can learn all about this exciting area at the Safford BLM office or website.

## Queen Valley/Montana Mountain - Superior, AZ

Trail Rating: Moderate 4-5

Trail Type: Loop

Trail Length: 46 miles

Approximate Time: 4-5 hours

Best Season: Spring-Fall

Traffic: Moderate to Heavy

Trailhead Coordinates: 33.276112, -111.276634

For an enjoyable but non-stressful trail ride, embark on this loop close to Gold Canyon, Arizona. Typically seen as a moderate route that most off-roaders can handle without any major difficulties. This path offers a fantastic high desert loop for SUVs and ATVs, reaching over 5,000 feet with breathtaking desert and mountain vistas. This location is a hot spot for camping, mountain biking, and off-road driving, meaning you'll probably run into other folks during your adventures. The trail is accessible all year and offers stunning views no matter where you go.

This challenging path up the mountain features several river crossings. A majestic forest of towering pine trees crowns the summit of the mountain. The descent is full of twists and turns, so beware of other drivers. The final stretch features a speedy and spacious dirt road.

Directions to trailhead: From the Florence Junction, take Highway 60 east, then turn left on Queen Valley Road a quarter mile past milepost 214. After 1.7 miles, turn right on Hewitt Station Road, which is State Route 357. Continue for another 3.1 miles, then turn left on State Route 172, and you will arrive at your starting point.

This trail has earned a spot on the Dangerous Roads blog for being so challenging. You can get trail maps, conditions, and difficulty on both the OnX Offroads and AllTrails+ app.

## Four Peaks OHV Area - Fort McDowell, AZ

Trail Rating: Main Trail Easy 2 with some side spurs Moderate 5-6

Trail Type: Main trail is out and back, with several spur trails that run off from it.

Trail Length: Main trail is a little over 20 miles one way

Approximate Time: 3-4 hours

Best Season: December - April

Traffic: Moderate to Heavy

Trailhead Coordinates: 33.669383, -111.495794

Enjoy an enjoyable off-roading experience through some of the state's most picturesque regions on this largely easy trek. Less than two miles from Brown's Peak, the trail starts in the high desert. It concludes in the high forest area. Since off-roading and scenic driving are highly popular in this area, you'll probably run into other visitors while exploring.

The great part of this area is that there is much more to this excursion than just the one road leading to the Four Peaks trailhead. When it comes to off-road vehicles of all kinds, this area is like a massive playground. Indeed, you might easily lose a whole weekend exploring the area's many dirt roads and trails.

Directions to trailhead: Just before the 204-mile marker, turn right onto Forest Road 143 from Highway 87. There is plenty of space to park and unload unregistered vehicles for the first mile or so. Several routes veer off to the south, connecting to the "Rolls OHV Area," a massive network of roads extending south to Saguaro Lake.

The GAIA GPS app provides maps of the area. You can also find out more in the Arizona offroad website at https://azoffroad.net/rolls-ohv-area.

## Cinder Hills OHV Area – Flagstaff, AZ

Trail Rating: Easy 2 - Difficult 8

Trail Type: OHV Recreation Area

Trail Length: 13,500-acres

Approximate Time: Varies

Best Season: Summer and Fall

Traffic: Moderate to Heavy

Trailhead Coordinates: 35.328054 -111.523053

Many off-road enthusiasts enjoy visiting the Cinder Hills since it is such a unique and unusual recreation spot. This region is distinguished by its exceptional landscape, which is derived from the presence of multiple volcanic cinder cones and craters that are encircled by a ponderosa pine forest habitat. The trails in this area are as diverse in difficulty as the unusual landscape that surrounds them.

Directions to trailhead: Travel on US 89 northeast of Flagstaff, about 7 miles north of Flagstaff Mall. Proceed straight east on FR 776.

Find out all the information on The Cinder Hills OHV Area at the Coconino National Forest office and website. You can also get maps of the location on the Avenza Maps app.

There are certain rules that are specific to the Cinder Hills Off-Highway Vehicle Area, they include the following:

- All vehicles on Frontage Roads 776 and 777 must be street legal.

- Helmets are required for all riders under the age of 18.

- All off-highway vehicles are required to have a US Forest Service approved spark arrestor.

- The recreation area does not permit the use of any containers made of glass.

## Lake Havasu ORV Network – Lake Havasu City, AZ

Trail Rating: From Easy 3 to Hard 7

Trail Type: OHV recreation area

Trail Length: 20 different off-road trail networks of varying lengths

Approximate Time: Varies

Best Season: October-April, Open year-round

Traffic: Varies

Trailhead Coordinates: 34.254255, -114.160942

Are you ready for a grand variety of off-road adventures? Then Lake Havasu is the place to visit anytime from Autumn through Spring. It is still open in the summer if you like temperatures that match Hell itself. There are over 20 different off-road trail networks in and around Lake Havasu City, offering a variety of terrains such as sand dunes, canyons, and open desert. This part of Arizona has a plethora of off-road trails to offer enthusiasts, all within driving distance, for an exciting weekend getaway in the state.

No matter what you're driving - a 4WD truck, dirt bike, sand rail, ATV, UTV, or any other vehicle - they all will provide plenty of pleasure when you're out on one of the many trails found here. Take your time to wander around, try some rock crawling if you're adventurous, or go all out and experience the excitement of speeding through off-road terrain.

Many of these exciting Arizona off-road trails will take you close to attractions like old mines and deserted mining towns. Although intriguing to investigate, these regions can be dangerous as not all mine shafts are labeled, so be careful when riding near mining areas.

The Arizona Game & Fish Department offers a wealth of information on off-roading in and around Lake Havasu City. This includes vehicle guides, safety education, off-road safety videos, and educational courses for recreational off-road vehicles.

You can find all about the trail system at  BLM Lake Havasu office or website.  The Avenza Maps app offers maps for all these trails free on their app.

The address for Buckskin Mountain State Park is at 5476 AZ-95, Parker, AZ 85344.

**Here is a list favor trails in this area:**

- **Gray Eagle Mine Trail**
    - Difficulty: Moderate 4
    - Trail Type: Loop
    - Trail Length: 5 miles
    - Approximate Time: 3 hours
    - Best Season: Fall to Spring
    - Traffic: Low
    - Trailhead Coordinates: 34.214222, -114.152444

    Set amidst the untamed Buckskin Mountains, this trail presents an opportunity for seclusion, as the moderately difficult drive keeps most people at bay, however it has grown popular with off-highway vehicles. There are several side paths to explore, some of which are rather challenging, but the majority of the 5-mile loop is on moderate terrain.

- **Falls Springs Wash Trail**
    - Difficulty: Moderate
    - Trail Type: In and out
    - Trail Length: 10 miles
    - Approximate Time: 7 hours
    - Best Season: Fall to Spring
    - Traffic: Low
    - Trailhead Coordinates: 34.52102, -114.27246

    The Falls Springs Wash OHV Trail is a moderate round-trip trail that provides scenic views of the surrounding area. You'll need a vehicle with high clearance for this trail. This trail is perfect for hiking and off-road driving, and chances are you won't run into many other people while you're out and about. You'll need a high-clearance SUV for this trail.

- **Crossman Peak**
  - Difficulty: Moderate to Hard
  - Trail Type: Loop
  - Trail Length: 14 miles
  - Approximate Time: 7 hours
  - Best Season: Fall to Spring
  - Traffic: Low
  - Trailhead Coordinates: 34.52113, -114.27256

  This trail winds through the isolated desert near Crossman Peak which is the highest peak in the area. While the majority of the path is easy, there are some tight spots and a couple of rocky areas that might pose a challenge to the less experienced driver. Navigation along this trail may prove challenging due to the lack of clear markings. You'll need a high clearance 4WD for this trail. It is unlikely you will run into many other individuals.

- **Cat Tail Cove to Rovey's Needle OHV Trail**
  - Difficulty: Moderate
  - Trail Type: End to end
  - Trail Length: 19 miles
  - Approximate Time: 4 hours
  - Best Season: Fall to Spring
  - Traffic: Low to Moderate

○ Trailhead Coordinates: 34.33337, -114.13613

This trail runs alongside Cattail Cove State Park. Search for a spot with gravel beneath the power line. Follow the trail leading to the Bill Williams River and the renowned Rovey's Needle rock formation. The trail offers a variety of landscape and plenty of chances for bird watching if you are so inclined. Through the use of bypass options, you can choose an easier ride over the most difficult portions of the terrain–but what's the fun in that. This location is a hotspot for both stock 4X4s and non-street legal ORVs. There is a spacious staging area suitable for motorhomes and large camping units at the trailhead. Don't miss the enjoyable climb to Rovey's Needle; it's quite interesting. There are plenty of different landscapes with numerous offshoot paths. The most common and accepted path meanders through a sandy wash with occasional large rock obstacles.

## Monument Valley Scenic Drive

Trail Rating: Easy 2

Trail Type: Loop

Trail Length:  13.5 miles

Approximate Time:  1-3 hours

Best Season: March - May, and September - October

Traffic: Moderate

 Trailhead Coordinates: 36.9852 -110.11351

This drive is not for the adventure, but for the sheer beauty and wonder of the area.   Driving through the Monument Valley Navajo Tribal Park is a must-do experience for anyone who loves the beauty of the Southwest.  The distinctive buttes and sandstone towers have always captured the attention of photographers, filmmakers, and western artists. While this drive offers a visual feast that would make even the slickest advertising posters look dull.. It's worth the drive, not because you'll conquer treacherous terrain, but because you'll conquer your own peace of mind, embracing tranquility while respecting our great outdoors.

This straightforward loop trail is widely regarded as one of the most iconic and stunning routes for any outdoor enthusiast to explore. This trail is well-visited, yet you can find moments of peace during off-peak hours.  Any all-wheel drive and four-wheel drive vehicles can handle this road easily, and 2WD vehicles with any decent clearance should handle the main road without any problems.

To enjoy this drive, you will need to travel into the Monument Valley Navajo Tribal Park also known as Tse'Bii'Ndzisgaii by the Navajos (which is like a national park for the Navajo people), using trail maps and driving directions available at the park office. There is a small fee to enter the park, and you can follow a self-guided route in your own vehicle. If you want to explore the remote areas of the park, you will need to take a guided Jeep tour. Only licensed vehicles are permitted in the park, and all off-road driving is prohibited. Make sure to check out the modern visitor center and museum. You can find a complete range of services that include lodging, an RV/campground, trading post/grocery store, available in nearby Gouldings, Utah.

Directions: When traveling from Kayenta on  US Highway turn Right (South) at the circle onto Monument Valley Road toward the "Monument Valley Tribal Park".   After making that turn east from there, you will soon see the big View Hotel and parking lot. The entry kiosk for the 17 mile scenic drive is downward and left of the hotel and that parking lot.

You can get a map on Gaia GPS, Avenza, plus directions, photos, and more on the Alltrails+ app.

## Capturing the Majesty: No Filters Required

I chose to save Monument Valley as my final trail to explore in Arizona. The experience of driving along the Monument Valley Scenic Drive feels like a much-needed break from the constant rush of life. It's a lighthearted reminder that encourages you to embrace the joy of the journey. As off-road enthusiasts, it's easy to become fixated on the level of difficulty and occasionally overlook the sheer beauty that envelops us. This hidden gem is a true marvel of nature's boundless creativity, demonstrating that the value of an adventure is not determined solely by the difficulty of the journey.

If you're a person who loves Instagram, then you're in your element. But here's a little tip: even the most amateur photographer can capture postcard-perfect shots, because, in Monument Valley, the landscape does all the heavy lifting. There's a rock formation at every turn flirting with your camera lens to take a picture.

If you can tell, I love the pure beauty that can be found in Monument Valley. Every time I visit the area, I feel like the area has rolled out a red carpet made of sandstone for everyone to enjoy its geological splendor.

## Last Thoughts On Arizona

When traveling in the Arizona frontier, remember that it has some very unique landscapes, everything from the high mountains near Flagstaff to the blistering deserts around Tucson. When off-roading here, always be prepared for the unexpected. In Arizona's diverse climate, weather conditions can change in an instant. One moment you might be roasting under the sun, and the next, a sudden storm could roll in, creating flash floods out of nowhere. Pack layers to stay comfortable in various temperatures and bring along essentials like water, snacks, and a first-aid kit. It's better to have them and not need them than to need them and not have them. And as always, Leave no trace of your journey except for tire tracks and memories.

So keep your eyes on the sky, your hands on the wheel, and your spirits high. With the right preparation and a touch off-road wisdom, you'll conquer Arizona's trails like a seasoned pro.

# Chapter 5:

# Finding the Best Trails and Trail

# Systems in Colorado

Colorado is the ideal location to enjoy the grandeur of the great outdoors while off-roading because of its breathtaking scenery, hilly terrain, and expansive open areas. You will be treated to breathtaking views as you explore the  diverse landscapes of iconic natural landmarks such as the Colorado Rockies or the Colorado National Monument near Grand Junction.

Western Colorado and Grand Junction offer breathtaking opportunities for off-roading, suitable for all skill levels. Grand Junction offers breathtaking landscapes that cater to both relaxed and daring adventures, allowing you to choose your preferred experience.

The more straightforward trails in this region provide stunning scenery and a satisfying day of riding. If you're thinking about off-roading in Colorado, you'll have plenty of options to pick from.

**Colorado OHV Permit Rules**

To operate in Colorado, an OHV must have one Colorado OHV permit or a current, valid Colorado Registration Card with two

Decals. This covers when traveling, in staging areas, on public land, and on trails designed for off-highway vehicles.

Every non-resident OHV is required to have a single, current, bright green OHV permit that is either carried on the vehicle or prominently displayed.

Off

Note that even plated, street-legal vehicles—resident or not—must have a Colorado OHV permit in order to drive on any publicly owned recreationally approved OHV trail or open space. Either the owner must carry the non-stick bright green OHV Permit or the permit sticker needs to be correctly placed on the car. This applies to cars registered in Colorado as well as other states.

**Lets Get Ready To Roll**

There is no question love off-roading in Colorado. It has so many amazing mountain trails and old historic mining roads, and scenic vistas to keep your love of adventure filled with excitement. Your driving abilities may  also be put to the test by a variety of obstacles as you take on the challenging terrain found in this beautiful state. If you're ready to elevate your off-road adventure, then let's go…

## Black Bear Pass (FS Road 648)- Telluride, CO

Trail Rating: Difficult 7

Trail Type: Point to point

Trail Length: 12 Miles

Approximate Time: 3 hours

Best Season: August - September

Traffic: Low

Trailhead Coordinates: 37.8967125,-107.7135511

This road is usually regarded as a difficult trail. It is perfect for off-road driving, and you probably won't come across many other people during your exploration. Plan ahead, since this road usually has snow that lasts into July.

This challenging road in the San Juan Mountains of Colorado will put even the most experienced drivers to the test. Several years ago there was a sign at the trailhead that stated, "You don't have to be crazy to drive this road - but it helps." Because of its challenging and somewhat notorious reputation, it has earned the Jeep Badge of Honor, and this trail definitely lives up to its reputation as one of the most perilous trails in the nation.

Directions to trailhead: From the town of Ouray, head south on US-550/Main St for 13 miles to the summit of Red Mountain Pass. Then turn right onto Forest Service road # 648 at the parking area. This is the trailhead for the Black Bear Pass road. From Silverton, take US Highway 550 north. At Red Mountain Pass, turn west on Forest Road 823 to get to the top.

You can view GPS trail maps, conditions, waypoints, and much more information on the following off-road apps; OnXOffroads, Trails Offroads, Gaia GPS, and AllTrails+.

## Imogene Pass (FS Road #869) - Ouray, CO

Trail Rating: Moderately Hard 6-7

Trail Type: Point to point

Trail Length: 18 miles

Approximate Time: 4-5 hours

Best Season: Summer-Fall, closed Winters

Traffic: Moderate

Trailhead Coordinates: 37.93929, -107.80637

In Colorado, which has an abundance of natural beauty, we think it's reasonable to say that the San Juans are among the most picturesque areas. Imogene Pass is a prime example of stunning natural beauty, featuring rock tunnels, cliffs, steep slopes, and breathtaking views from 13,000 feet above sea level.

This is truly an exceptional experience. You'll be exploring one of the most historic mining areas in the state. The Tomboy Ghost Town and Camp Bird Mine, with decaying buildings and other mining relics, provide additional scenery along the way. Make sure to stick to the path.

2WD and low-clearance vehicles should not attempt to drive on this road.  To drive this road, you should have a 4×4 high clearance vehicle and be an experienced driver. Unlicensed OHV vehicles are only allowed to travel the road east of Marshall Creek over the Ouray county line.  Plan your trip accordingly because the road is accessible from May 16 to November 30. Up until early July, there's a chance that snow will block the road. If you find it hard to focus on the road, just pull over, alright?  Because nobody wants to be picking up pieces of you and your vehicle at the bottom of the canyon.

Directions to the trailhead: It is best to start in Ouray, Colorado and end in Telluride.  From Ouray, proceed southward along US-550 S/3rd St/Main Street to Camp Bird Road and then proceed for 4.7 miles. Turn right onto County Road 26 and proceed for a distance of 1.3 miles. Make a left turn and cross the stream. This is the beginning of the Imogene Pass road.

This trail has earned its place on the Most Dangerous Roads blog.  You can view GPS trail maps, conditions, and difficulty on both the OnX Offroads and AllTrails+ apps.

# Alpine Loop - Ouray, CO

Trail Rating: Moderate 4 to Difficult 7

Trail Type: Loop

Trail Length: 65 miles

Approximate Time:  8 hours

Best Season: Summer-Fall, closed Winters

Traffic: Moderate

Trailhead Coordinates: 37.988709, -107.649670

Colorado's Alpine Loop scenic and historic byway is only snow-free from June to September. This scenic drive takes you through a breathtaking landscape from beautiful aspens and pines to treeless tundra above treeline and mountains that look like they've been painted with red and yellow splashes near Ouray, Lake City, and Silverton.

This route winds its way through cascading mountains as you cross over two mountain passes. Located to the north, Engineer Pass reaches an elevation of 12,000 feet, offering an exceptional viewpoint for capturing photographs of the impressive Uncompahgre and Wetterhorn peaks, each exceeding 14,000 feet in height. On the more southern route, Cinnamon Pass also tops out at 12,000 feet and provides views of some of the nation's highest mountains — Handies, Sunshine and Redcloud peaks.

Keep in mind that the entire route is suitable for 4x4 vehicles, as it is considered a Jeep Badge Of Honor Trail. If you're driving a family sedan, you need to switch to a higher-clearance vehicle before tackling this impressive route.  Many parts of this trail are single vehicle passage, so always be careful, and give the right of way to those making their way up the mountain. This trail is worth every awe-inspiring minute, but it is not for the faint hearted.  So gather your courage, and keep your eyes on the road.

76

It has several segments that can be taken as part of the Alpine Loop, or on their own. You can see each of these roads on any off-road app or via paper maps. These segment trails are:

- Engineer Pass
- Cinnamon Pass
- Stony Pass
- Hurricane Pass

Directions to trailhead: From Ouray, travel south on Main Street until it turns into the Million Dollar Highway. Stay on the MDH for 3.9 miles. There is a small parking area on the left side of the road which is the trailhead.

You can view GPS trail maps, conditions, and difficulty on the AllTrails+ app.

## Ophir Pass - Ophir, CO

Trail Rating: Moderate 4-5

Trail Type: Point to point

Trail Length: 10 miles

Approximate Time: 4-5 hours

Best Season: Summer-Fall

Traffic: Moderate

Trailhead Coordinates: 37.84767, -107.72483

Ophir Pass Road poses a moderate challenge for off-road enthusiasts. Much of the trail requires high clearance vehicles, but is relatively easy, except for one difficult section located on the western side of the pass, where there is an extremely narrow and rocky shelf. Here, inexperienced drivers may find passing to be a bit daunting. During the summer, Ophir Pass can be navigated by most high clearance vehicles, but drivers need to be cautious and attentive on the narrow parts of the road.

This scenic route is not just a beautiful way to travel between two beloved mountain towns, Telluride and Silverton. Southwest Colorado is famous for its top-notch off-roading opportunities, although many of the trails in the region are quite challenging. Although it has its fair share of difficulties (especially for those who are afraid of heights), Ophir Pass is a more manageable trail, even though it is considered a Jeep Badge Of Honor trail.

Unregistered vehicles are permitted on Ophir Pass Road to the east of Ophir town, but are not allowed to drive through the town.

Directions to trailhead: Look for County Rd #8 located on Highway 550, about 5 miles north of Silverton. There is a wide gravel road that heads west just before mile marker 75.

You can view GPS trail maps, conditions, and difficulty and more on any of these three apps; OnXOffroads, or Alltrails+, or TrailsOffroad.

## Wagon Wheel OHV Trails System – Meeker, CO

Trail Rating: Easy 2 - Difficult 9

Trail Type: 16 different trails

Trail Length: 250 miles of trailways

Approximate Time: Varies on what trail you take

Best Season: Summer-Fall

Traffic: Moderate

Trailhead Coordinator: 35.572611, -117.550629

The town of Meeker, Colorado boasts the Wagon Wheel OHV Trail System, which features more than 250 miles of trails and sixteen interconnected loops within the White River National

Forest. It is an off-road lovers paradise with the opportunity to explore a diverse range of challenging mountain paths, encounter a variety of wildlife, and visit numerous historical and cultural landmarks. The trail system provides breathtaking views and a range of trail challenges to cater to riders of all abilities.

Both Rio Blanco County and the town itself are known for their accommodating attitude towards OHVs, permitting travel on city streets and specific county roads.

**Here is the QR code for complete guide to all Meeker trails.**

Complete directions for all the main trails found in the Meeker area can be found by downloading the Wagon Wheel trail guide at: https://meekerchamber.com/wp-content/uploads/2019/07/WagonWheel_2019Guide.pdf

Here are ten of the most challenging and most popular trails available at this off-roading paradise:

- **Miller Creek Loop**

  - Trail rating: Moderate 4

  - Trail Type: Loop

  - Trail Length: 33 Miles

  - Approximate Time: 4 hours

  - Trailhead Coordinates: 39.932442, -107.770925

  - This trail provides miles of fun for at least moderately experienced drivers with OHVs no more than 62 inches wide. This ride features a few somewhat difficult brief sections, the most notable of which is a steep and slightly rocky downhill section that is half a mile long. It is recommended that riders have prior experience riding trails that feature steeper, rocky, off-camber, and narrow features.

- Directions to trailhead: From Meeker travel East 1.6 miles on Market St, then turn right onto County Road 8 for 10.4 miles. Then turn Right (South) onto CR 57 for 1 mile to the parking area.

- Route Directions: Start at the Miller Creek Parking Lot, then CR57, FS215, FS214, FS2211, FS211, FS216, FS2216, FS217, FS2200, FS218, FS215, CR56, then return to Miller Creek Parking Lot

- **Sleepy Cat Peak**

  - Trail rating: Moderate 4 to Moderately Difficult 6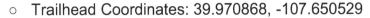

  - Trail Type: Out and Back

  - Trail Length: 24 Miles

  - Approximate Time: 2.5 hours

  - Trailhead Coordinates: 39.970868, -107.650529

  - There is little doubt that Sleepy Cat Peak is one of the most identifiable features in Meeker. The trail features a few short portions that are steep, rutted, off-camber, and/or highly rocky, as well as several tiny stream crossings. There are no width restrictions, however high-clearance vehicles are a must to tackle this trail.

  - Directions to trailhead: From Meeker, take CR 8 for 20 miles to the Lake Avery Parking Lot.

  - Route Directions: Start at the Lake Avery Parking Lot, then CR115, FS250, FS280, FS290, FS250, CR115, and return to the Lake Avery Parking Lot.

- **Fawn Creek to Deadhorse Loop**
  - Trail rating: Moderate 4 to Moderately Difficult 6

  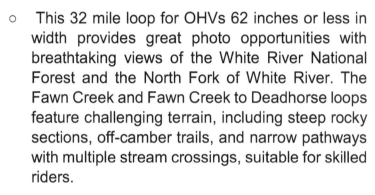

  - Trail Type: Loop
  - Trail Length: 32 Miles
  - Approximate Time: 4.5 hours
  - Trailhead Coordinates: 40.033420, -107.530764
  - This 32 mile loop for OHVs 62 inches or less in width provides great photo opportunities with breathtaking views of the White River National Forest and the North Fork of White River. The Fawn Creek and Fawn Creek to Deadhorse loops feature challenging terrain, including steep rocky sections, off-camber trails, and narrow pathways with multiple stream crossings, suitable for skilled riders.
  - Directions to trailhead: The trailhead is located 26.5 miles up County Road 8 from Meeker at the Fawn Creek/County Shop Parking Lot.
  - Route Directions: Begins at the Fawn Creek Parking Lot, then take CR8, CR115, FS280, FS290, FS293, FS1809.2, FS231, FS230, and CR8 will take you back to Fawn Creek Parking Lot.
- **Fawn Creek Loop**
  - Trail rating: Moderate 4 to Difficult 7

  - Trail Type: Loop
  - Trail Length: 28 Miles
  - Approximate Time: 4 hours

- Trailhead Coordinates: 40.033420, -107.530764

- This loop is for seasoned riders with OHVs needing to measure 62 inches or less in width. It is perfect for experienced riders who are seeking a shorter day ride with technical challenges. This loop is sure to please as it winds through hills and valleys filled with stunning wildflower fields. This trail involves challenging terrain such as steep, rocky paths, off-camber trails, and narrow passages with small stream crossings.

- Directions to trailhead: The trailhead is located 26.5 miles up County Road 8 from Meeker at the Fawn Creek/County Shop Parking Lot.

- Route Directions: Begins at the Fawn Creek Parking Lot, then take CR8, CR115, FS280, FS290, FS292, FS2292, FS2270, FS250, FS2271, FS285, FS280, FS289, FS2289, FS2236, FS235, CR52, then take CR8 back to the parking lot.

- **Pagoda Peak Loop**
  - Trail rating: Easy 3 to Difficult 7
  - Trail Type: Loop
  - Trail Length: 28 Miles
  - Approximate Time: 3.5 Hours

  - Trailhead Coordinates: 37.44652, -107.1191

  - This trail is for OHV's 50 inches or less in width. Experienced riders can enjoy the thrill of conquering this 20-mile loop and take in a plethora of amazing views! Head over to the parking lot at the FS230 turnoff to start your journey and take in the stunning views of Ripple

Creek Pass along the Flat Tops Scenic Byway. This journey features sections of steep, extremely rocky, off-camber, and narrow pathways, along with small stream crossings.

- Directions to trailhead: Start and finish at Ripple Creek Trailhead Parking Lot, up County Road 8
- Route Directions: FS1804, FS230, CR8

- **Flat Tops Scenic Adventure Ride**
  - Trail rating: Easy 2
  - Trail Type: End To End
  - Trail Length: 82 Miles
  - Approximate Time: 3 hours

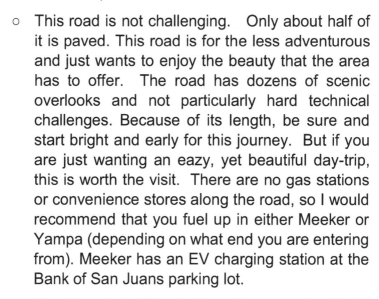

  - Trailhead                Coordinates: 40.15773, -106.90871
  - This road is not challenging.    Only about half of it is paved. This road is for the less adventurous and just wants to enjoy the beauty that the area has to offer.   The road has dozens of scenic overlooks and not particularly hard technical challenges. Because of its length, be sure and start bright and early for this journey.   But if you are just wanting an eazy, yet beautiful day-trip, this is worth the visit.   There are no gas stations or convenience stores along the road, so I would recommend that you fuel up in either Meeker or Yampa (depending on what end you are entering from). Meeker has an EV charging station at the Bank of San Juans parking lot.
  - Directions to trailhead: From Yampa, take CR 17 west out of town.

- **Yellow Jacket Historic Trail**
  - Trail rating: Moderate 4 - 5
  - Trail Type: Loop
  - Trail Length: 43 miles
  - Approximate Time: 4-5 hours
  - Trailhead Coordinates: 40.147777, -107.740107

  - This ride is for OHV's no wider than 62 inches and with good ground clearance. Riders can discover the area's fascinating history as you travel through the historic Uranium Peak Mining District and past the Milk Creek Battlefield Park on this loop. The path to Aldrich Lake provides breathtaking scenery. This ride includes challenging sections with rocky terrain, uneven surfaces, and bumpy trails.
  - Directions to trailhead: From Meeker, drive or trailer on CR 15 (approx 14 miles) to the Yellow Jacket Pass Parking Lot at the junction of CR 15 and CR 48.
  - Route Directions: From the parking lot, travel on CR48, FS250, FS260, FS263, FS2633, FS2214, FS2286, FS2267, FS260, FS2278, FS250, FS251, FS2279, FS252, CR51, returning to the Yellow Jacket Pass parking lot.

- **Hay Flat to Miller Creek Loop**
  - Trail rating: Easy 1 to Moderate 3
  - Trail Type: Loop
  - Trail Length: 60 miles (23 on paved roads)
  - Approximate Time: 3 hours

- Trailhead Coordinates: 40.042933, -107.908884
- This trail is a great ride for anyone with a reliable 4X4 and some basic experience on rocky, uneven terrain. A favorite trail among the locals, where you can navigate a series of switchbacks as you ascend into hillsides and valleys filled with beautiful wildflowers and stunning views. About half of the drive will take place on well-maintained gravel and paved roads, while the rest will be on Forest Service 4x4 dirt roads.
- Directions to trailhead: Trailhead begins (835 Sulphur Creek Rd) the Meeker Fairgrounds parking lot.
- Route Directions: From Fairgrounds travel south on 1st St, to Market St. then turn South onto 10th St. At the fork in the road, take CR13, then on to CR38, FS211, FS214, FS215, CR57, CR8, then onto the Connector Trail.

- **Yellow Jacket to Sleepy Cat Loop**
  - Trail rating: Difficult 7
  - Trail Type: Loop
  - Trail Length: 45 miles
  - Approximate Time: 4 hours
  - Trailhead Coordinates: 40.147777, -107.740107
  - This ride is for OHV's no wider than 62 inches and with good ground clearance. This ride takes you past the famous Sleepy Cat Peak as you meander through stunning open spaces and weave through beautiful pine forest. This trail is a rollercoaster of a ride that features brief

stretches of difficult, steep, extremely rocky, uneven, tilted, and/or narrow paths. It's important for riders to have experience with these type of trail conditions.

○ Directions to trailhead: From Meeker, drive or trailer on CR 15 (approx 14 miles) to the Yellow Jacket Pass Parking Lot at the junction of CR 15 and CR 48.

○ Route Directions: From the parking lot, travel on CR48, FS250, FS260, FS2272, FS250, FS270, FS2270, FS2292, FS292, FS290, FS250, FS2278, FS250, CR48 returning to parking lot.

- **Miller Creek to Elk Creek Loop**

  ○ Trail rating: Moderate 4 - Difficult 8

  ○ Trail Type: Loop

  ○ Trail Length:  32 Miles

  ○ Approximate Time: 4.5 hours

  ○ Trailhead Coordinates: 39.932442, -107.770925

  ○ This ride is only for experienced riders in an OHV's no wider than 62 inches with good ground clearance.  This loop, follows Miller Creek and offers a stunning view of the Elk Creek valley, is an ideal ride for those who are more experienced. Enjoy a breathtaking view of the area upriver. There are a number of lengthy, steep, rocky climbs with rutted and off-camber parts as well as a long, steep, rocky descent for riders.

  ○ Directions to trailhead: From Meeker travel East 1.6 miles on Market St, then turn right onto County Road 8 for 10.4 miles. Then turn Right (South) onto CR 57 for 1 mile to the parking area.

- Route Directions: Start at the Miller Creek Parking Lot, then take CR57, then onto FS215, FS214, FS212, FS2212, FS212, FS214, FS211, FS216, FS2162, FS218, FS215, and CR57 back to the parking lot.

To learn all about this extensive trail system at the wagonwheeltrails.org website or by using the Avenza app.

## Gold Belt Scenic Byway

This scenic byway is a paved road that is worth seeing. The Gold Belt Scenic Byway winds through the gold belt of Colorado.

With numerous routes including well-known highways and byways like Phantom Canyon Road, Shelf Road, High Park Road, and Teller County Road 1, this byway is about one hour from Colorado Springs. Big sites like Phantom Canyon, the Royal Gorge, and Pikes Peak will also be visible to you.

Phantom Canyon Road is one of the main thoroughfares that links Cañon City and Victor on the Gold Belt Tour. This section features two tunnels and three elevated bridges, and it passes through Phantom Canyon. There is enough to view.

This scenic byway has two great off road adventures that is great for anyone, but especially for less experienced drivers

1. **Phantom Canyon Road - Florence, CO**

   Trail Rating: Easy 2-3

   Trail Type: Point to point

   Trail Length: 32 miles

   Approximate Time:  2-3 hours

   Best Season: Summer-Fall

   Traffic: Moderate

Trailhead Coordinates: 38.43780, -105.11343

The Phantom Canyon Road is typically seen as a route that presents a moderate level of difficulty because of some rough dirt sections combined with narrow roads beside sheer cliffs, but the truth is any stock AWD or 4WD vehicle can easily handle this road. The trail meanders through a picturesque canyon, utilizing rugged, one-way tunnels, narrow openings carved into the mountainside, and a unique curved bridge. Beware, there are sheer cliffs in the area for those who are afraid of heights.

If you're looking for a place to get some peace and quiet when it's not as busy, this road is a great choice since it is one of the most beautiful and historically important roads in Colorado. This rough, beautiful road goes from Cañon City to Victor. It goes through Phantom Canyon and gains 5,500 to 9,500 feet in elevation.

Directions to trailhead: From Cañon City, CO travel East on CR 123 6 miles. Then turn North on CR 67 (across from the Fremont County Airport).

You can view the GPS trail map, difficulty and more on the Alltrails+ app.

2. **Shelf Road - Cripple Creek, CO**

   Trail Rating: Easy 2

   Trail Type: Point to point

   Trail Length: 27 miles

   Approximate Time: 2 hours

   Best Season: Summer-Fall

   Traffic: Low

   Trailhead Coordinates: 38.742761, -105.176288

Shelf Road offers a thrilling and only slightly challenging drive as you navigate through limestone cliffs with winding roads. The road is named due to being carved out of the canyon wall and ascending several hundred feet in certain spots. Shelf Road is a challenging and hilly route that any AWD can handle. This trail is perfect for hitting the dirt roads and enjoying the beautiful views, with a low chance of running into other folks during your adventure.

Directions to trailhead: From Cripple Creek follow CO-67 South, then turn right onto Xenia St/Teller County Rd 88 which turns into the Shelf Rd/CR 88.

You can view the GPS trail map, conditions, and difficulty and more at both the OnXOffroads app or the Alltrails+ app.

## Grand Mesa Trails System, Grand Junction, CO

Trail Rating: Easy 2 - Difficult 9

Trail Type: 40+ different trails

Trail Length: 150+ miles of trailways

Approximate Time: Varies on what trails you take

Best Season: Summer-Fall

Traffic: Varies on what trails you take

Trailhead Coordinates: Multiple entrances, use the QR code below to access all trails.

**Here is a QR code to a map that shows all the following trails:**

If we didn't mention Grand Mesa OHV trails, would this really be a book about off-roading? Grand Mesa offers a wide variety of 4x4 trails, ranging from easy and enjoyable to

demanding and difficult. Grand Mesa offers a variety of natural features that create an exciting playground for both you and your vehicle.

Explore the ATV trails of the Grand Mesa National Forest, which provide 150 miles of thrilling adventures for your ATV, OHV, and 4WD vehicle. The paths wind through lush forests with many lakes, fields of tall grass and wildflowers, and dense clusters of Aspen, Spruce, and Douglas fir trees.

There are both beginner-friendly roads and challenging trails wind through the region just south of Mesa and Collbran. The more challenging trails feature rock crawling, water crossings, mud holes, rocky climbs up some foreboding hillsides. However, if you are not that daring, fear not, the majority of the trails are situated on the flat-top mountains and leisurely meadow rides that are much less demanding. The Grand Mesa offers a variety of fun for riders at every level; and if you love fishing, you can try your luck fishing in one of the 300 lakes on Grand Mesa.

**All The Main Trails On The Grand Mesa Trails System (found via QR code):**

Porter Cutoff #535
Cedar Mesa #718
Hawxhurst #530
Buzzard Park #519
East Brush Creek #504
East Leon #730
Ella #732
Aqueduct #753
Eureka Cutoff #734.1A
Hightower #524
Kimball Creek #532
Last Chance #731
Owens Loop #539
Point Camp #725
Porter Mountain #534
Ridge #646
Salt Creek #514
Silver Spruce #517

Monument #518
Power Line #520
Scotland #752
Boundary #525
High #515
Buzzard #536
Trout Lake #743
Beaver #516
Hay Park #729
West Green Mountain #719.1A
Triangle Stomp #736
Two Peak #521
West Salt Creek #513
Willow Reservoir #755
Divide Forks Campground - Grand Valley RD
Divide #523

Elk Park #720
Drop Off #726
Smalley Mountain #531
Greenwood #721
Green Mountain #719
Little Dolores #648
Brush Creek #529
Burn #522
Youngs Creek Connector #508
Crum Reservoir #511
Eureka #734
Battlement #527
Bonham #512
Boundary Cutoff #526
Bull Basin #507
Carpenter #510

You can learn more about these trails and get maps and other information at either of these placess:

Grand Valley Ranger District

218 High Street P.O. Box 330

Collbran, Colorado 81624

970-487-3534

Rifle Ranger District

0094 County Road 244

Rifle, Colorado 81650

970-625-2371

## A Few Last Thoughts About Colorado

"Stay the Trail" is the off-roading motto for Colorado. This maxim doesn't limit the amount of fun you can have when exploring the wilderness in a Jeep tour, ATV, or other off-highway vehicle (OHV) because there are so many different and exciting trail options.

For off-roaders in Colorado, there is a website entitled Staythetrail.com. It is a great interactive OHV route map, that can become an invaluable asset to help you find hundreds of trails to ride. It displays every trail system in the state, and you can click on any point on the map to view additional information on any particular trail.

Colorado has so many amazing trails, that there are entire books just about all that this great state has to offer. But since this book only has one chapter, I am having to leave off some of the other amazing trails that are available. However, it would take years for you to just get through the trails that I have listed in this chapter. So ride on, be safe, and have fun!

In conclusion, if you are someone who enjoys experiencing new things and are thinking about going on a trip to Colorado, you should definitely take advantage the off-roading experiences available to you. With that in mind, pack your bags so you can hit some of the many beautiful trails, and be ready for an experience that you will never forget!

# Chapter 6:

# Finding the Best Trails and Trail Systems in Idaho

Idaho's beauty is best seen in its huge backcountry, where trails that span thousands of miles take you through a wide range of nature areas. I may be prejudiced having lived in Idaho for several years, but I believe the abundance of routes in Idaho is some of the best for off-roading enthusiasts. During your next trip to the Gem State, make sure to stop by some of these wonderful places.

## Idaho OHV Permit Rules

According to the Idaho Department of Parks and Recreation, residents and non-residents who ride off-highway vehicles (OHVs) throughout the state are now required to get an OHV sticker. As of the date of this publication, there is a $12 fee for residents and non-residents. On the Idaho Department of

Parks and Recreation website, everyone can obtain their OHV registration sticker.

## St. Anthony Sand Dunes Recreation Area - Saint Anthony, ID

Trail Rating: East 1 to Hard 7

Trail Type: Sand dunes that range from 10' to 400' high

Trail Length: About 35 miles long and 5 miles wide of dune trails

Approximate Time:  As long as you can ride

Best Season: Summer-Fall

Traffic: Moderate to High

Trailhead Coordinates: 43.96292, -111.85365

As a kid growing up in Southeastern Idaho, I spent my fair share of time up on these dunes.

The St. Anthony Sand Dunes contain almost 10,000 acres of sand dunes, with dune heights that range from 10 to as high as 400 feet.  They attract ATV and OHVs sand bashers and other off-road aficionados in from June into late fall.  The "Big Dunes" are closed to motorsports from January through May since wildlife such as elk, deer, and grouse winter there.  The Small Dunes are open year round.

West side huge dunes like Choke Cherry, Devil's Dunes, and Dead Horse Bowl offer challenging steep riding for even the best riders. The Red Road Area Access is the easiest way to reach the smaller dunes on the east side which provide a wonderful experience for less adventurous

riders. Centrally located, Egin Lakes is the nearest entry point to Thunder Mountain (Crapo's Hill) with both smaller and larger dunes. Sand Hills resort is on the east side of the sand dunes and open year-round (though winters can be snowy). To protect winter habitat west of Thunder Mountain and Egin Lakes, the huge dunes are restricted.

Any vehicle on the dunes must have a 6"x12" orange or red flag at least 8 feet from the ground. Also, a spark arrestor is required.

Directions to trailhead: The dunes are easy to find by driving 8 miles directly west on Heman road out of St. Anthony. You can also get great information about the dunes area by googling the term, BLM, St. Anthony Sand Dunes. There is a fee if you use the camping area.

## Payette National Forest OHV Trails - McCall, ID

Trail Rating: East to  Hard 2-8

Trail Type: Loops, Point to Point, and more

Trail Length: Various lengths

Approximate Time:  Depending up which trail you take

Best Season: Spring-Fall

Traffic: Low to Moderate

Trailhead Coordinates:  Follow this QR Code to get all 80+ OHV trails can be found at the Payette National Forest website.

I did not choose this area because of an amazing OHV trail, but rather the sheer number of off-roading trails you can enjoy. With over 80 designated OHV trails, this area is a virtual off-roader's paradise, providing trails that accommodate any rider from beginning to hard core rock crawlers.  There are so many incredible opportunities to explore in the Central Mountains, filled with boundless meadows, alpine lakes, as well as both the

Payette and Snake Rivers. These mountain communities are brimming with beautiful scenery and untamed areas that will provide days of enjoyment should you want to stay that long.

**Here are three of the best trails in the Payette National Forest:**

### Ruby Meadows, Loon Lake and Duck Lake - McCall, ID

Trail Rating: Hard 7

Trail Type: Out and Back

Trail Length: 48 miles

Approximate Time:  20 hours

Best Season: May - October

Traffic: Moderate

Trailhead Coordinates: 45.25545, -115.89852

To enjoy this trail you should plan on camping out since it takes two full days to complete. It's generally regarded as a difficult route.  Even though this is a well-liked trail for fishing, trekking, and camping, you can still find some peace and quiet during the slower parts of the day.   While in the area, you should take a little time an enjoyable swim in the Burgdorf Hot Springs about 1.8 miles North of the trailhead.

Directions to Trailhead: From McCall, take the Warren Wagon Rd 28.8 miles to the trailhead.  It will be on the right side of the road with a small parking area.

This location is best laid out at the AllTrails+ app.

### Jump Creek/Sand Basin OHV Trail - Marshing, ID

Trail Rating: Moderate 4

Trail Type: Loop

Trail Length: 24 miles

Approximate Time:  6 hours

Best Season: Spring-Fall

Traffic: Low

Trailhead Coordinates: 43.48008, -116.92379

The Jump Creek/Sand Basin OHV Trail is a moderately challenging route. This trail is open year round, however Spring through Fall are the best seasons. Make sure you have your camera ready because you will come across breathtaking sites such as canyons, waterfalls, deserts, mountain forests, and possibly even a herd of wild mustangs. It is recommended to travel this trail as a group in case you get into trouble.

Directions to Trailhead: From Marshing, ID, go West on Main Street, then at the Chevron, turn South on US-95 (I.O.N. Hywy 456) to Poison Creek Grade Rd. From Poison Creek Grade Rd turn lef on Jump Creek Road to the Jump Creek Trailhead parking lot.

You can find maps and directions to the trailhead on the AllTrails+ app.

## Rocky Canyon Road OHV Trail - Boise, ID

Trail Rating: East 2-3

Trail Type: Point to Point

Trail Length: 12 Miles

Approximate Time: 1-2 hours

Best Season: Spring-Fall

Traffic: Low

Trailhead    Coordinates:    43.61552,    -116.18191

You can explore the Rocky Canyon Road from March to October. The majority of the route is unpaved, making it suitable for both novice and expert off-roaders; however, for more experienced drivers, the trail divides into more rugged terrain. You'll get breathtaking views of the nearby lake and river from either portion of the trail that you take.

This point-to-point trail is ideal for mild off-road driving. You probably won't run across many other travelers while exploring this road, which can make for a wonderfully peaceful drive. Be aware that early spring rains and snow runoff can create some quite deep ruts, but a standard 4x4 can manage this trail without much trouble.

Directions to Trailhead: The trailhead is found at the corner of East Reserve St and Shaw Mountain Rd in Boise.

You can find maps for the Rocky Canyon trailhead on both OnXOffroad app, and the AllTrails+ app.

### Louie Lake Trail - McCall, ID

Trail Rating: Moderately Hard 5-6

Trail Type: Out and Back

Trail Length: 5 Miles

Approximate Time: 4 hours

Best Season: May - October

Traffic: Moderate

Trailhead Coordinates: 44.869401, -115.973579

The Louie Lake Trail is popular for all kinds of off-road adventurers from spring into late fall. Enjoy the stunning scenery of Eastern Idaho's mountainous terrain. You can locate the Louie Lake Trail in the beautiful Payette National Forest, not far from McCall. Just a heads up before you start; the path to the trailhead is quite rough and challenging. Begin your journey from the starting point along Boulder Lake Road. From this point, you will travel towards the south along the Louie Lake Trail. Heading into the woods, the trail will slowly ascend into an area filled with a variety of mountain plants and animals.

This road leads you through some of Idaho's prettiest areas, and you will end at the beautifully serene Louie Lake. Much of the trail is a fire road, and it is well worth the journey, but you need either AWD, 4WD, or OHV with sufficient clearance to travel the road.

Directions to Trailhead: From McCall take South 3rd St, then head east on Durham Ln/Elo Rd. Continue right to stay on Durham Ln/Elo Rd until it turns east into Boulder Lake Rd, which will end at the trailhead just before Boulder Meadows Reservoir.

There are parts of this trail that may seem confusing, so I recommend that you get a map from the local BLM office. AllTrails+ provides a printable PDF map or off-line map that will also help.

## Silver City Road - Nampa ID

Trail Rating: Moderately Easy 3

Trail Type: Out and Back

Trail Length: 21 Miles

Approximate Time: 2 hours

Best Season: June - October

Traffic: Moderate - Heavy

Trailhead Coordinates: 43.15848, -116.50881

The road to Silver City starts easy, but then gets a little rougher. There are steep climbs and tight turns on the road as it winds deeper into the beautiful southwestern Owyhee mountains. One part of the road has steep, twisting turns that lead down to Sinker Creek. There is a fair amount of traffic on this road during the summer, so be careful as you approach the hidden spots.

The road goes up from Sinker Creek and into the woods. There are some rocks on this dirt road, so high-clearance SUVs are better than cars for getting through them. You should be ready for more hairpin turns as the road goes over the top of the hill and down to the public toilets. The road goes up almost 4,000 feet.

The best part of this road is getting to see the ghost down of Silver City.  It is Silver City is unique because it is one of the few old mining towns in the west that has not either burned down or become commercialized. It's like going back in time when you step in this town.  I personally love this trip, not only because of the beautiful countryside, and Silver City, but the other old ghost towns and multiple aged, abandoned cemeteries sprinkled throughout the area.

Directions to Trailhead:  From Nampa, travel south on ID-45 until it forks left onto ID-78 E (Marsing Murphy Rd) until you pass the village of Murphy.  4.8 miles after Murphy, turn right onto Long Rdg Rd/Silver City Rd.

Add some fun to the trip by returning via Silver City Rd & Long Rdg Rd.

Gaia GPS has a downloadable map, and the Trails Offroad app provides a map and pictorial waypoints.

## Challis Creek Lakes Trail #4268 - Challis,ID

Trail Rating: Moderately Easy 3 - 4

Trail Type: Out and Back

Trail Length: 8 Miles

Approximate Time: 2 hours

Best Season: April - October

Traffic: Moderate

Trailhead Coordinates: 44.51805, -114.43353

Challis Creek Lakes Trail #4268 is a Jeep trail west of Challis. At Mosquito Flat Reservoir, the Challis Creek Lakes path begins. It leads to three beautiful alpine lakes in the Frank Church-River of No Return Wilderness area. This rugged, bumpy, and uneven trail with several creek crossings winds through the forest with stunning mountain views.

This trail is fairly easy to navigate if you have a high clearance vehicle with good all-terrain tires and preferably 4WD. It provides a beautiful, while slightly challenging trip into Idaho's wilderness country.

Directions to Trailhead: From Challis head north on 7th St toward Main St/Yankee Fork Rd for 10.4 miles. Turn Left onto Challis Creek Rd for 6.3 miles (becomes Forest Rd 40091) which becomes the trailhead.

This trail can easily be tracked using the TrailsOffRoad app which has pictorial waypoints to help make sure you are not lost.

## Cinnabar Mine and Mill OHV Trail - Cascade, ID

Trail Rating: Moderate 4

Trail Type: Out and Back Loop

Trail Length: 86 Miles

Approximate Time: 10-15 hours

Best Season: May - October

Traffic: Low

Trailhead Coordinates: 44.653602, -115.549945

This wonderful trail heads out not far from Yellow Pine, Idaho. This mountain trail is generally considered to be moderately difficult. Off-road driving on this trail is great, and you won't likely run across many other visitors while exploring. The trip is definitely worth the journey, so make sure to set aside a couple of hours to walk through the old mine area. Many of the old buildings are still mostly intact providing a look in the the past. The old mill is still standing, but the roof is collapsing. Other buildings have crumbled, but overall, this mine and surrounding area with well worth visiting, with dozens of amazing opportunities for Kodak moments (for those of you under 30, that means "great selfies").

There are several sections of the road that are very narrow, with some places that are very rough, and a few where landslides have made the trail fairly narrow. However, any driver with experience and either an OHV or 4X4 should do fine.

Because of the length of this trail, you may consider camping overnight along the way.

Directions to Trailhead: Take ID-55 to the north end of Cascade, ID, then turn right onto NF-22/Warm Lake Rd (becomes FSR-474) for 16.4 miles. The trailhead is at the junction with Johnson Creek FR 413 and FR 479U1.

If you want a more difficult ride, check out the Monumental Summit to Thunder Mountain to Cinnabar Mine OHV Trail. You can find out about this ride on AllTrails+.

## Lucky Lad Mine - McCall, ID

Trail Rating: Moderately Hard 5 - 6

Trail Type: Out and Back

Trail Length: 61 Miles

Approximate Time: 6-8 hours

Best Season: May - October

Traffic: Low

Trailhead Coordinates: 44.65328, -115.55086

The Lucky Lad Mine is located inside the Frank Church-River of No Return Wilderness area, but can be accessed via a high clearance 4X4 or OHV via the Artillery Dome route.

Plan on a solid six to eight hours to traverse this out-and-back trail. It is usually seen as a moderately difficult ride. Off-road driving on this trail is excellent, but you should go with an experienced driver. There are some short switchbacks, a narrow shelf road near the top, and two beautiful saddles. There are two or three major burn scars along some of the trail. A short, steep trek is required to reach the mine after you arrive.

Directions to Trailhead: (you will use the same route as Cinnabar Mine and Mill OHV Trailhead) Take ID-55 to the north end of Cascade, ID, then turn right onto NF-22/Warm Lake Rd (becomes FSR-474) for 16.4 miles. The trailhead is at the junction with Johnson Creek FR 413 and FR 479U1.

Directions to the mine are hard to find, so the best option is to use a combination of the Onxmaps app combined with the AllTrail+ app.

## Pinyon Peak - Stanley, Idaho

Trail Rating: Moderate 3-4

Trail Type: Out and Back

Trail Length: 26 Miles

Approximate Time: 4 hours

Best Season: May - October

Traffic: Low

Trailhead Coordinates: 44.396041, -115.167323

This impressive peak stands tall at an elevation of 9,947 ft in Custer County. It's up there among the highest roads in Idaho. Nestled in the Salmon-Challis National Forest, it is right in the heart of Idaho. This moderately challenging trail to the peak is completely unpaved. The road is known as Pinyon Peak Loop Road (NF-172). You should plan ahead since the drive can feel like a marathon. It is a fairly demanding drive that should be tackled with a 4x4 vehicle. This road has earned a place on the website dangerousroads.org, which should tell you a little about this road. It is quite off the beaten path, so make sure to take necessary precautions and rely on your good judgment to go when the weather is good and that you go early enough in the day so as not to travel back down the mountain after dark.

The journey to the top is over 26 miles, traveling from NF-008 (Seafoam Road) to Loon Creek Road. The final stretch to the summit includes eight sharp hairpin turns on a steep incline that can pose a challenge, so it's best to use low range for the last portion to the summit.

Directions to Trailhead: From Stanley, ID travel west on ID-21 N for 18 miles. You will come upon a junction for FR 40008 and Lola Creek Road. Turn right onto Forest Rd 40008. This will take you past Beaver Creek Campground on your way up to the peak.

The GAIA GPS app provides a mapping to the peak. You can also find a few videos on YouTube if you want to preview the drive before you take it.

## Last Thoughts About Idaho

Having grown up in Idaho, I believe that Idaho's beauty is best seen in its huge backcountry, where trails that span thousands of miles take you through a wide range of natural areas. Idaho is truly a captivating destination, a true haven of untouched wilderness that has inspired countless artists, dreamers, and adventurers. The truth is, there aren't many places better than Idaho for off-roading adventures.

# Chapter 7:

# Finding the Best Trails and Trail Systems in Montana

**Forget the Beaten Path, Montana's Waiting with Wild, Wheelin' Wonderland!**

Montana is known for its wildlife and beautiful scenery. As you drive across Montana, you will see everything from foothills to badlands, prairies, and world-famous mountains. It's amazing how different the surroundings are in just one state.

## Montana OHV Permit Rules

On all public lands in Montana, riding on authorized motorized routes and trails requires an OHV Trail Pass. An OHV Resident Trail Pass, good for two years, is available to residents. Nonresidents can get a Nonresident Temporary Use Permit, and it is good for a whole year.

## Looking for Fun In Montana

If you thought Montana was just about big skies and larger-than-life steaks, strap in for a surprise that'll rumble your 4x4's undercarriage! In this chapter, we're going to look at someplace that will have you itching to hit the road. Montana is an off-roader's paradise, where each trail tells a tale of earth's rugged splendor and your vehicle is the journal for writing your ongoing adventures.  Here are a few locations that can help you to add more pages to your off-road history.

### Ringing Rocks Trail - Butte, MT

Trail Rating: Moderate 5

Trail Type: Out and Back

Trail Length: 9 Miles

Approximate Time: 4 hours

Best Season: May - October

Traffic: Moderate

Trailhead Coordinates: 45.903421, -112.226039

A brief and enjoyable path with a range of challenges. The first two-thirds of the trail is fairly easy, but after you pass the halfway point, there are a few places that can pose a challenge to less experienced drivers. You need a high-clearance 4x4 or OHV to make the last third of the trip since the road has rocky sections and some deep holes that will bottom out any regular car.  There is a water crossing that varies in depth from 1 to 3 feet depending on the season. There's usually a way around most challenges, but there's one narrow spot where full-size SUVs or trucks might scrape if not careful.  There is one area with a steep, technical wash area that requires a good spotter. There is a bypass route for those who are less experienced.

To get the full experience of the trip, bring a hammer.  There is a very interesting phenomenon in this area that can only be found in seven areas worldwide.  The rocks actually ring like a bell when they are struck with a hammer or similar instrument. Trust me, this is so cool to hear the sounds that come from these rocks.

Directions to Trailhead: Taking Exit 241 (Pipestone) off of I-90, proceed east for roughly three-quarters of a mile on a gravel road (parallels interstate), then turn north on a gravel road, cross the railroad tracks, and continue north for about three miles.

You can find maps and other information about this trail on both AllTrails+, and onX Offroad apps.

## Fairy Lake via Fairy Creek Trail - Bozeman, MT

Trail Rating: Moderate 4

Trail Type: Out and Back

Trail Length: 5 miles

Approximate Time:  2.5 - 3 hours

Best Season: May - October

Traffic:  Moderate

Trailhead Coordinates: 45.90888, -110.92820

Situated in the Bridger Mountain Range, Fairy Lake may be reached by the Fairy Creek Trail, making it a fairly popular location. The trail, generally rated as moderately difficult, takes between two and a half to three hours to finish. Although it's a popular trail, there are still peaceful spots, especially in the slower parts of the day.

The route to the trailhead can be extremely rough and sometimes quite muddy, so keep that in mind. Depending on the season, you will need a 4WD with plenty of clearance.

Directions to Trailhead: From Bozeman, travel Hwy 86/Bridger Canyon Road north.  Continue traveling for about 21 or 22 miles.  Go five miles on Fairy Lake Road (Forest Road #74) to the west (left). Proceed to the large dirt parking lot on the right. Fairy Lake Campground and Fairy Lake are nearby.

You can find a map and other details on the AllTrails+ app.

## Elkhorn and Crow Peak Trail - Boulder, MT

Trail Rating:  Moderately Difficult  5

Trail Type:  Out and Back

Trail Length: 8

Approximate Time:  2 hours

Best Season:  Summer-Fall

Traffic: Moderate

Trailhead Coordinates: 46.27652, -111.94343

This single-lane trail passes by Glendale Butte and Big Mountain and traverses the Helena National Forest. You will pass by several camp spots and the Mission Lookout Picnic Area as you drive alongside Crow Creek. There are several types of wildlife in the area, including bears, moose, elk, and deer.  It is a beautiful forest with breathtaking views all along the way. As long as you stay on the road and close all gates you go through, you are permitted to cross any private property. You can explore historic mining sites, abandoned cabins, and so forth.

The first portion of the road is considered to be an easy drive; it is only the last portion that becomes more challenging. For the first portion, you should at least have an AWD with decent clearance, but you will need a high-clearance 4X4 of OHV to make the entire journey.

This moderately used trail gains 2,844 feet in elevation, so it has some steep areas along the way.  Between May and October, this road often has hikers on it, so be careful and watch for people on the road.

Directions to Trailhead: Head south on MT-69 for 5.9 miles to White Bridge Rd.  After crossing the bridge, turn right onto Lower Valley Rd for 2 miles. At the fork in the road, take the left fork onto Elkhorn Rd.  Follow the road to Elkhorn Ghost Town

State Park. The trail begins at the northeastern end of Main Street in Elkhorn Ghost Town State Park.

This trail can be found on both the AllTrails+ and OnX Off-road apps.

## Daisy Pass OHV Route - Cooke City, MO

Trail Rating:  Moderately Easy 3-4

Trail Type:  Out and Back

Trail Length: 11.5

Approximate Time:  2 hours

Best Season:  Summer - Fall

Traffic:  Moderate

Trailhead Coordinates: 45.02404, -109.91751

This 4WD road is tucked away in the Beartooth range. It has many characteristics that come to mind when considering the high alpine environment, including summer wildflowers, glacial snow masses, crystal-clear streams, and granite pinnacles. Daisy Pass offers all of this, plus an abundance of hiking trails for those who want to enjoy this beautiful wilderness on foot.

The Daisy Pass trail road was first used as a mining road in the late 1800s and early 1900s. Despite the fact that it is not a hard drive, you will need a high-clearance 4x4 vehicle to travel this road. Be aware that it is usually closed and completely impassable from November to May. It is a pretty steep trail and often has some deep ruts, particularly in the spring.

At the peak, there are very few historic remnants of the New World Mining District remaining.

Directions to Trailhead: Trailhead begins about ½ mile east of Cooke City off from Beartooth Hwy. Turn left (north) onto Daisy Pass Trail Rd.  Daisy Pass Trail #404 begins at Forest Service Road 552,

You can find maps and more about this scenic road on Gaia GPS, AllTrails+, and TrailsOffroad apps.

### Hungry Horse Reservoir Scenic Loop - Hungry Horse, MT

Trail Rating: Easy 1-2

Trail Type: Loop

Trail Length: 170 miles

Approximate Time:

Best Season: June - September

Traffic: Low

Trailhead Coordinates: 48.386191, -114.051761

This road is not known for how challenging it is, but rather how beautiful the drive is. Situated on the Flathead National Forest, high in the Rocky Mountains, Hungry Horse Reservoir is a true hidden gem, spanning 34 miles and boasting roughly 170 miles of shoreline. The roads surrounding this lake are mostly made of gravel or dirt, with about 14 kilometers being paved. This driving loop takes you across the South Fork of the Flathead River and along the shores of Hungry Horse Reservoir, surrounded by beautiful mountains.

It's still a local favorite, only minutes from Hungry Horse and Columbia Falls, as well as Glacier National Park. There are plenty of opportunities for hiking, boating, swimming, fishing, camping, and of course some fun 4WD-friendly dirt roads. You will find several beautiful waterfalls in this area. There are no services besides Forest Service campgrounds with vault toilets and boat launches. There is also no cell service around most of the lake. If you choose to drive the entire loop, you should make sure you have a full tank of gas. The best times to visit this trail are July through August. It is also worth considering bear spray since there are a lot of black bears and some grizzlies in the area.

Directions to Trailhead: From Highway 2 in Hungry Horse turn south on Hungry Horse Dam Rd/NF-895.

## Hedges Mountain via Cave Gulch - East Helena, MT

Trail Rating: Moderate 3

Trail Type: Out and Back

Trail Length: 17.5 miles

Approximate Time: 3 hours

Best Season: Summer - Fall

Traffic: Low

Trailhead Coordinates: 46.665951, -111.693203

This area is fairly well-known for its difficult terrain. This adaptable track offers a comparatively isolated experience for those who enjoy being alone when they off-road.  This trail offers really stunning vistas! It gets more and more beautiful the higher you go. There are, however, some challenges to be mindful of, the road is quite narrow in some areas,with loose gravel and shale, and some off-camber areas. Much of the trail also consists of extremely steep inclines and declines.  Also be aware if the weather is inclement that the slate rock areas can become extremely slick.

Please keep in mind that this trail is mostly intended for ATVs, so if you are wider than 50" and not careful, you may leave a little paint behind.  However, some people who have gone up in full-size SUVs have said they found it manageable.

This trail is geared for experienced drivers and OHVs, trucks, Jeeps, or SUVs.  Stock SUVs can handle this road, however no one should ever consider taking a normal sedan up this trail.

Directions to Trailhead: From the address of 8015 Canyon Ferry Rd (Kim's Marina & Resort) take Cave Gulch Road north for 1 mile.

You can find more about this trail on the AllTrails+ App. There are also maps at the local BLM office.

## Benbow Jeep/OHV Road: East Fishtail Creek to Island Lake trail - Fishtail, MT.

Trail Rating:  Moderate 5

Trail Type: Out and Back Loop

Trail Length: 9 Miles

Approximate Time: 4 hours

Best Season:  May to October

Traffic: Low

Trailhead Coordinates: 45.396602,-109.737980

This trail is known as both Benbow Jeep Trail, Benbow OHV Trail, and Forest Service Road 2415.

This road has earned the name of being a Jeep or OHV trail because it definitely requires 4-wheel drive and sufficient clearance, and at least a moderately experienced off-road driver behind the wheel.

The trail takes you through meadows, streams, woodlands, and fairly rocky hillsides with some tricky switchbacks.  On this drive you will find some of the beautiful views that have made Montana famous with gorgeous valleys and roughed mountains, and then you will find the remnants of the Benbow Mine Headframe as a final reward for your journey.

Directions to Trailhead: The trail begins at the Benbow Jeep path trailhead off of Benbow Road, aka the Forest Service road 2414 or NF-1414.

You can find maps, pictures, and more on both OnX Offroad, AllTrails+, and there is a great brochure with a detailed map that can be found by googling the US Forest Service Benbow Jeep Trail.

## Blacktail Wild Bill OHV Trails system - Lakeside, MT

Trail Rating: Three trail options: Main Trail- Easy to Difficult 2-8; Trails 2 & 3 - Moderate to Difficult 4-8

Trail Type: Out and Back

Trail Length: 3 legs for a total of 20 miles

Approximate Time: 8 hours

Best Season: Summer - Fall

Traffic:  Low

Trail Coordinates: Main trail - 47.996204, -114.365810

This 20-mile ORV trail system is made up of three different trails.  The main trail begins off of Blacktail Mt. Road on Road #917a and intersects with the other two trails which begin off of Truman Creek Rd #213 and from the trailhead on Road #2990.

This trail starts on Road #917a from Blacktail Mt. Road and meets up with the other two trails that start on Road #213 from Truman Creek Rd and Road #2990 from the beginning.

In the summer, you can travel on the trail, and using the easy bypasses will keep the trail fairly easy. However, by not doing bypasses the trail is definitely difficult.  The difficult route has earned its place as a Jeep Badge Of Honor trail.

The Blacktail OHV system can be accessed from three different trailheads.

Trail #917 begins at Hwy 93 close to Lakeside. Turn west on Blacktail Rd. Immediately after turning, make a left turn in front of the hardware store. Proceed approximately 12 miles up

Blacktail Rd, which becomes Forest Service Rd #917. On the left lies the trailhead.

Trail #918 starts at the intersection of Highway 2 and Kila Hill Road in the village of Kila, then head east for .2 miles and turn right on Kila Road. Follow Kila Road for 1 mile and turn left on Smith Lake Rd. Follow this road for .3 of a mile and turn right on Browns Meadow Road. Follow that road for 1 mile, then turn left on Truman Creek Road. Then after 2.3 miles and turn right on Wild Bill Creek Rd. Follow Wild Bill Creek Rd for 9.4 miles and turn slightly left on Dayton Creek Rd which takes you to the trailhead.

Trail #919 begins at Hwy 2. Turn onto Kila Rd and travel approximately 1.8 miles. After passing through Kila, turn left onto Smith Lake Rd and travel approximately 2/10 miles. Next, turn right onto Browns Meadow Rd and travel approximately 1 mile. Finally, turn left onto Truman Creek Rd and travel approximately 2.3 miles. Continue up this road for approximately 2.7 miles and turn left down a seemingly private driveway for 1/10 of a mile. The trailhead is located on the right. On the left side of the drive is a wooden three-rail fence. You've veered just a bit too much if you pass a road on the left (#9662) with an open field on the right.

You can find this trail by individual sections on both the OnX Offroad and Trails Offroad apps.

## Pipestone OHV Recreation Area - Butte, MT

Trail Rating: Easy 2 to Difficult 8

Trail Type: Interconnected Trail System

Trail Length: Various Lengths

Approximate Time: Varies

Best Season: Summer - Fall

Traffic: Moderate to High

Pipestone Trailhead Coordinates: 45.91115, -112.24281

Homestead Trailhead Coordinates: 45.92273, -112.40992

This 30,000-acre travel management area is situated just north of I-90 and around 15 miles east of Butte. Riders of motorcycles, ATVs, and OHVs (50" wide or less) are drawn to this area. The routes are also used by mountain bikers.

The Pipestone Off-Highway Vehicle Recreation Area has 75 miles of trails and is close to Whitehall. The trails are spread out over more than 30,000 acres of land that used to be a mine area. There are many trailheads, staging spots, places to camp, and other things. It's easy to see why this place is so popular with people who like being outside.

Directions to Trailheads:

Pipestone Trailhead: Take the I-90 freeway exit # 241. Turn north onto Hot Springs Rd. The trailhead parking area is about 100 yards up the road on the right.

Homestake Trailhead: Take the I-90 freeway exit # 233. Turn north onto Homestake Pass Rd. The trailhead parking area is about 75 yards up the road on the right.

Both the Homestake and Pipestone trailhead parking lots provide dirt ramps to unload your machines.

You can learn more about this area by visiting the Pipestone OHV Area Facebook page. You can also get maps, waypoints, and additional information about the trails in this area from AllTrails+, TrailForks, OnX Offroad, and Avenza Maps.

## Shepherd Ah Nei SRMA (Special Recreation Management Area) - Billings, MT

Trail Rating: Easy 2 to Difficult 8

Trail Type: Interconnected Trail System

Trail Length: Various Lengths

Approximate Time: Varies

Best Season: Summer - Fall

Traffic: Moderate to High

Trailhead Coordinates: 46.03459, -108.28387

Out of the 1,062 acres, around 50 miles of trails are reserved for off-road vehicle use. Note that many of the trails are limited to vehicles 50" wide or less. Large grasslands, ponderosa pines, and junipers lead to spectacular views at this popular recreation site.

If you are bringing multiple vehicles, you will need to purchase a separate recreation permit for each vehicle at the self-service kiosk located in the parking lot. Be sure to check the weather forecast before you plan to visit, as the region may be closed due to rainy and muddy conditions. A $5 day pass can be obtained at the on-site kiosk, or at the Billings BLM Field office.

Directions to Trailhead:

From the old Kmart in Billings Heights, head east on Highway 312. After 7.7 miles, turn left into Shepherd Road at the blinking light. Proceed north 4.78 miles to Scandia Road. After 2.6 miles, turn left onto CA Road after making a right onto Scandia Road. About 4.6 miles further on the left is the OHV parking area.

## Final notes about off-roading in Montana:

Montana offers amazing trails and a plethora of backwoods adventures for off-road enthusiasts of all levels. If you are an overland traveler, Montana runs the gamut from backcountry and boondocking spots to developed campgrounds with tent sites and all the amenities you might need  for your camping. An off-road adventure is a thrilling and unbelievable way to see the beautiful highlands and wilderness of Montana.

For those of you who are not well acquainted with the weather of Montana, the winters are often very cold, and often last into March and April. Some trails do not even open until June, so make sure to plan ahead, and pack warm clothes. Even in the summer, the evenings can get chilly. Montana is truly a place to enjoy the great outdoors.

# Chapter 8:

# Finding the Best Trails and Trail Systems in Nevada

There are thousands of miles of dirt roads, trails, and tracks that wind across wide valleys and desert canyons, calling out off-highway vehicle enthusiasts to explore Nevada. With 85% of Nevada  designated as unfenced public land, it is literally an off-road enthusiast playground.

There's no better place to take your OHV and test you and your machine's abilities than Nevada. With open valleys, desert canyons, over 300 mountain ranges, and many more areas are crisscrossed by thousands of miles of dirt roads, trails, and open desert, all calling for you to come ride.

## Nevada OHV Permit Rules

In order to legally operate in Nevada, almost all OHVs with a displacement higher than 70cc and those produced in 1976 or later need to be registered and have a registration decal on them. An annual registration fee of $20 is required. Applications are welcome, and decals can only be sent out via mail. If your vehicle is licensed for on-road use, you do not need to get an OHV decal.

**Get Ready For The Fun**

In this chapter, we will explore some of the best and most interesting trails and trail systems that Nevada has to offer. Let's see some of the fun available:

## Rocky Gap Trail - Las Vegas, Nevada

Trail Rating: Difficult 7

Trail Type: Straight Through

Trail Length: 8 Miles

Approximate Time: 4 - 5 hours

Best Season: Spring - Fall

Traffic: Moderate

Trailhead Coordinates:  36.131857, -115.421463

Rocky Gap route in Clark County, Nevada, is a highly challenging backcountry route. This road is very rocky and rough as it winds its way through part of the Red Rock Canyon National Conservation Area.  This road is definitely not for the faint of heart or beginning off-road drivers.  Even experienced drivers need spotters to overcome the challenges of this trail. It has earned its place on the Jeep Badge Of Honor list and is also on the DangerousRoads.org blog.

To drive this trail, you must have a high-clearance 4WD vehicle or OHV, plus you should have a high-lift jack, shovel, tow rope, and a friend.

Directions to Trailhead: Rocky Gap Road has entrances on the east and west.  The Red Rock Canyon National Conservation area is the route that leads to Rocky Gap Road from the east. Take NV-159, often known as West Charleston Blvd., west off I-215 West.  Turn right onto Red Rock Visitor Center Rd. after 5.2 miles.

You can find maps, waypoints, pictures, and more on OnX Offroad, AllTrails+, Trails Offroad, Trailforks, and Gaia GPS apps. It can also be found on MapQuest and Google Maps.

## Gold Butte Backcountry Byway - Bunkerville, NV

Trail Rating: Moderately Easy

Trail Type: Out and Back

Trail Length: 63 Miles

Approximate Time: 4 hours

Best Season: Fall-Early Summer, Open Year Round

Traffic: Low-Moderate

Trailhead Coordinates: 36.73185, -114.21839

This road has a few challenges that require an AWD or 4WD vehicle with decent clearance since it has areas of deep sand. It is important to watch the weather before entering the Byway, since it can become impassable during inclement weather due to flash flooding.

The Gold Butte Backcountry Byway showcases Southern Nevada's most scenic vistas and the Anasazi, Paiute, and early American Miner history. The Gold Butte Backcountry Byway follows historic mining roads and cattle trails across the hills and washes of the area. You can enjoy seeing desert fauna, old petroglyphs, sinkholes, and some of the most amazing red and white sandstone formations that you will ever see. These wonders include thousands of petroglyphs, historic mining and pioneer-era artifacts, rare and threatened wildlife like the Mojave Desert tortoise and desert bighorn sheep, dramatic geologic features like sculpted red sandstone and rock spires, and fossil track-sites from 170 to 180 million years ago.

Directions to Trailhead: From I-15 take exit 112. Turn south on Riverside Road/NV-170 N for 3 miles. Turn Left (west) onto

Gold Butte Rd. The trailhead is the parking area immediately on your left.

You can find maps, pictures, waypoints, and more on both the AllTrails+ and Trails Offroad apps. Gaia GPS and Avenza both have maps that you can download.

## Valley Of Fire OHV Loop - Overton, NV

Trail Rating: Moderate 4

Trail Type: Loop

Trail Length: 22 Miles

Approximate Time: 3 hours

Best Season: January - April, Sept-November

Traffic: Moderate

Trailhead Coordinates: 36.59707, -114.4895

This moderately challenging road is a popular off-roading trail for anyone who knows the area. The Valley Of Fire trail offers truly breathtaking views for anyone who loves the red rock areas of the Southwest. You can also find petroglyphs along the way, and interesting side trails to explore.

The trail's terrain has a fair amount of washboarding, and areas with deep sand that require high clearance. It's best to explore the path during the week to avoid the weekend crowds.

Directions to Trailhead: From the center of Logandale Moapa Valley Blvd turn west on W. Liston Ave to the end of the street, then turn right onto N. Mills Street.

You can learn about this specific trail the AllTrails+ app

## Logandale Trails System (Valley Of Fire) - Logandale, NV

Trail Rating: Varies from Easy 3 to Very Difficult 8

Trail Type: Varies

Trail Length: Varies

Approximate Time: Varies

Best Season: Autumn, Winter, Spring (Summer gets very hot)

Traffic: Moderate to High

Trailhead Coordinates: 36.593457, -114.526805

Interconnected with the Valley Of Fire area are more than 200 miles of trails in the Logandale Trails System (LTS). These trails can be used by all types of off-road vehicles. The LTS covers more than 45,000 acres and has a lot of amazing places to ride. There are trails for riders of all skill levels, and some are only for expert riders.

This trail system is a popular spot for recreationists in the southern Nevada area. Many of the trails are good for most types of OHVs, however, some trails are too narrow for standard sized vehicles, while others require specially modified SUVs and Jeeps to handle the extreme range of driving required.

There are camping areas if you want to spend multiple days in the area. Weekends and holidays become very crowded. Weekdays are the best times to visit this area.

Different trails from the Logandale Trails System are found on most of the off-road apps including OnX Offroad, AllTrails+, Trails Offroad, TrailForks, Gaia GPS and Avenza.

To get to the Logandale Trails, take exit 93 off from I-15 in Nevada, then take Nevada Hwy 169 toward Logandale/ Overton. Turn right on Liston Rd. and follow that road to the right, until you cross a railroad track. Once you have done that, follow the road that directs you into the LTS.

Directions to trailhead: Take Nevada Hwy 169 toward Logandale/Overton from I-15. Take Liston Rd. to the right. Proceed straight ahead on the road and cross the railroad tracks. Observe the path leading to the LTS.

Maps of the area are available at the BLM office or online at the Logandale BLM website.

## Hungry Valley Recreational Area, aka "Moon Rocks" - Reno, NV

Trail Rating: Easy 2 - Difficult 8

Trail Type:  Varies

Trail Length:  Varies

Approximate Time: Varies

Best Season: Spring - Fall

Traffic: Moderate to High

Trailhead Coordinates: 39.848886, -119.74127

The Hungry Valley Recreational Area is one of the best areas to test your independence as an off-road enthusiast . Situated between Pyramid Lake and north of Reno, this vast network of trails is overseen by the Nevada Bureau of Land Management (BLM), providing access for off-roading, rock climbing, and other activities in this surreal terrain.

This area is better known locally as the "Moon Rocks" because of its massive, house-sized, smooth granite rock formations. The Travel Nevada website says that the location gives off the impression that you're off-roading on the moon.

This area offers a vast trail system that keeps riders of all skill levels engaged, from large open areas for beginners, to steep rocky climbs for advanced riders, and everything in between.

Almost every kind of off-road vehicle can explore these public lands. ATVs, dirt bikes, UTVs, quads, Jeeps, dune buggies, high clearance trucks, or any other off-road vehicle can have a blast at this lunar looking area.. Just remember to bring your sense of adventure, plenty of gas, and your favorite off-road vehicle.

Riding at Moon Rocks requires a Nevada OHV sticker. During the winter check ahead to make sure the area is open, since it does close occasionally due to extremely bad weather.

Directions to Trailhead: Follow Pyramid Hwy (State Route 443) north from Sparks' Interstate 80. After traveling 15.5 miles in a northwest direction, bear left onto Winnemucca Ranch Rd. Proceed about 4 miles to the staging area for the Hungry Valley Recreation Area, which is on the left.

Trails Offroad, Overland Bound, AllTrails+, Trailforks, Gaia GPS all provide maps and great info about this site. Both AllTrails+ and Trailforks list several of the trails in the area separately and rate them per difficulty. You can also find more about this location at thedyrt.com, TravelNevada.com, or the Nevada OHV website. The local BLM office also has some great maps of the area.

## Pony Express Trail - Nevada & Utah

Trail Rating: Easy 2-3

Trail Type: Point to Point, Overland

Trail Length: 550 miles

Approximate Time: 3-4 days

Best Season: Spring-Fall

Traffic: Low

Trailhead Coordinates: 40.230828, -112.184176

If you are up for a marathon drive, this is the trail for you. This 500+ mile route runs from Utah's West Desert at a town called

Fairfield, through the entire state of Nevada, ending in Carson City, Nevada. This trail is a real test of stamina for both the driver, passengers, and the vehicle. Even though this trail is rated as easy, and beginner divers can handle the trail, it still has its share of challenges. Any AWD and 4WD in good condition can drive this route easily, but should have good all-terrain tires since some sections have large gravel sections that can cause flat tires–trust me, I know from personal experience. Stock 2WD cars can usually travel this road, but may have some problems if bad weather sets in; the silt covered roads can become a muddy mess if you are caught out during a rain or snow storm.

The historic Pony Express Trail is one of the few public overland paths here in America. This path is as close as it gets to the old trail that mail carriers rode horses on more than 160 years ago.

This overland trip will take you three to four days. So make sure you bring plenty of food, gas, and don't forget (per my earlier note) a spare tire. There are sections of the Pony Express Trail that closed during the winter. During the summer and fall months the trail can become very dusty due to soft soil and silt fields. Be aware that many parts of the trail are out of cell service. Because much of this road is so far off the beaten path, it is suggested that travelers do not venture this road alone.

Directions to Trailhead: From I-15 take the Lehi Main St exit #279 and head west on Lehi Main Street. It will eventually turn into UT-73 W/W Cedar Fort Rd. Follow this road for 25 miles. Then take the paved road to the left. This is the E Faust Rd/Pony Express Rd. This is the official trailhead for the Pony Express trail heading Westbound.

You can find a map of the entire trail on Gaia GPS, OnX Offroad, and the BLM offices along the route. I recommend that you download the trail segments before you begin your journey.

You can also get the entire map of the Pony Express Trail if you are a premium member of the website, overlandtrailguides.com. It can be found at their following webpage:

https://www.overlandtrailguides.com/post/pony-express-trail

## Beatty to Goldfield Adventure Route - Beatty, NV

Trail Rating: Easy 2-3

Trail Type: Point to Point

Trail Length: 115 Miles

Approximate Time: 4 hours

Best Season: Spring - Fall

Traffic: low-moderate

Trailhead Coordinates:

Beatty to Goldfield (South to North): 36.891256, -116.751061

Goldfield to Beatty (North to South): 37.709349, -117.237415

The Beatty to Goldfield Adventure Route winds through scenic mountain and desert landscapes in Nevada. Mining roads and four-wheel-drive trails traverse the entire region, connecting Beatty and Goldfield. Starting in Beatty, the main trail heads north into the mountains to the long-gone settlement of Gold Point. There are the remnants of the ghost town, and you can actually stop and eat at a small restaurant/bar, and even sleep in one of the old mining cabins. This fun little"living" ghost town makes for a great rest stop along the way.

The trail then heads north from Gold Point to the small town of Goldfield and then on to Tonopah. Along the way, riders will pass numerous abandoned mining sites, stunning geological formations, forests of Joshua trees and cacti, and maybe even a few wild burros.

Because most of the roads are two-track dirt roads, high-clearance, four-wheel-drive vehicles are your best bet, however AWDs such as Subarus fare fine on these roads. Be cautious when traveling in the canyons or on the flats during rainy weather because roads may become impassable in some places.

The best place to get the map for this site is on either Avenza Maps or from the OHV Nevada website found on this QR code.

Directions to Trailhead:

From Beatty (South to North): Start at the Fluorspar Canyon Rd, which is approximately 1 mile south of Beatty on Highway 95.

From Goldfield (North to South): the trail begins on the west end of 4th Street in Goldfield. There is a staging area directly behind the Goldfield Visitor Center, off of Hwy 95/Veterans Memorial Highway and 1st Street.

Starting from Beatty, you can take Fluorspar Canyon Rd, which is conveniently located about 1 mile south of Beatty on Highway 95. The trail starts at the north end of the route in Goldfield, specifically on the west end of 4th Street. There is plenty of room for staging at the Goldfield Visitor Center, conveniently located off of Hwy 95 at 1st Street.

On the Beatty end of the trail, you will find dozens of great OHV trails that lead to another amazing ghost town of Rhyolite, plus other fun off-roading trails. Here are a few of the best trails in the area:

- **Rhyolite Railroad Loop & Ghost Town: Easy 2-3 (Great Ghost Town)**
  - Directions to Trailhead: In Beatty, 1.8 miles west of the intersection of US Highway 95 and Nevada Highway 374, turn right (north) on the broad unmarked road.
  - Trailhead Coordinates: 36.902999, -116.789618
  - This easy 4x4 trail follows a former railroad line. 4-wheel drive isn't necessary, but good ground clearance is. Aside from the two washout zones, there are grade cuts and fills. There is one washout that has to be followed by an existing bypass, and there is another washout that is roughly 300 feet long and somewhat rocky and uneven.

- **552 Mining Entry Road: Moderately Easy 3**
  - Directions to Trailhead: Travel northwest out of Las Vegas on US-95 N. Drive 45.3 miles from exit 93. The trail is on the left side of the road between mile markers NY2 and NY3.
  - Trailhead Coordinates: 36.59321, -115.94135
  - This is a simple gravel road with some washed-out areas and loose rocky areas. A 4x4 vehicle is recommended, however not mandatory. AWDs with decent clearance should do fine on this road.

- **Old Stagecoach Road: Moderate 4**
  - Directions to Trailhead: You need to follow the coordinates. The small parking area is just off US-95.

  - Trailhead Coordinates: 37.049250, -116.772000
  - This trail goes around Pioneer Mine and the hills. It has narrow, rocky two-tracks, graded parts, and even a sandy wash. There is a very faint two-track road that gets very narrow and can be hard to follow in one place.

There are more than dozens other off-road trails in the area. **Here is a PDF that outlines a dozen other local OHV trails to consider.**

Lucky Strike OHV Road - Las Vegas, NV

Trail Rating: Moderate 4

Trail Type: Straight Thru

Trail Length: 7 Miles

Approximate Time: 2 Hours

Best Season: Year Around

Traffic: Moderate

Trailhead Coordinates: 36.349578, -115.505232

Located just outside of Las Vegas, the Lucky Strike Road is an off-road trail that features some challenges that require four-wheel drive ability at the beginning and the finish of the trail. In the center of the course, is a pleasant, and not overly demanding drive. There are some camping sites along the way. It is a nice place to get away from the scorching heat of Las Vegas. The biggest challenges you will find on this trail are some moderate off-camber areas, narrow sections, deep sand, and wash-out areas.

Directions to Trailhead: Travel northwest out of Las Vegas on US-95N for 11 miles. When you come to Tule Springs Fossil Beds/Corn Creek Rd Kiosk Parking Area, turn left onto the dirt road on the west side of the highway. Travel west for exactly 5.7 miles. At the crossroads, turn left onto Lucky Strike Rd.

You can find additional mapping and other information about this trail on these apps; Trails Offroad, AllTrails+, OnX Offroad, and Gaia GPS.

## Sand Mountain, Fallon NV

Trail Rating: Easy 2 - Difficult 7

Trail Type:  Various

Trail Length:  Various

Approximate Time:  Various

Best Season:  Open year round.

Traffic:  Moderate - High

Trailhead Coordinates: 39.294036, -118.404730

Dune Bashers, here is another fun site for you. Sand Mountain Recreation Area is a 4,795-acre OHV fee site. Dune length is 3 miles and width is 1 mile, and offers off-road drivers a constantly shifting landscape. The main dune stands at 600 feet high. Open OHV use on unvegetated areas with just sand is allowed. In areas where there is vegetation, OHVs can only use designated roads and trails.

Despite being on the "loneliest road in America" this is a very popular area that attracts 50,000–70,000 guests annually. This site has a set of rules that you need to obey when riding on the dunes. Visit the BLM website for fees and requirements.

Directions to Trailhead: From Reno, take Highway 50 toward Fallon. Sand Mountain lies directly north of Highway 50, just 25 miles east of Fallon.

There is a fee for $40, which is good for up to 7 days. For someone who is a frequent rider, an annual pass costs $90.

## Silver State Trail - Lincoln County, NV

Trail Rating: Easy, Moderate, Difficult

Trail Type: Loop

Trail Length: 260 miles (plus multiple side trails)

Approximate Time: Varies

Best Season: Spring and Fall

Traffic: Moderate

Trailhead Coordinates: 37.66060, -114.763445

The small communities of Caliente, Alamo, Pioche, and Panaca Nevada are home to several trailheads for the Silver State Trail, an off-highway vehicle adventure route that has received national recognition for being the first Congressionally-designated off-highway vehicle trail that covers over 260 miles of wild backcountry terrain in central Nevada. There are numerous side trails that interconnect the Silver State trail between the four communities, the town of Mesquite, and the state border with Utah. The main route is clearly marked with signs that indicate its length and points of access. Along the Great Basin Highway are staging areas and access roads. You can find lodging, supplies, food, and fuel in each of the towns. There are several places to camp in the four local state parks.

All of the main Silver State Trail can be accessed with full-size 4WD vehicles; however, there are some optional sections that are limited to ATVs under 50 inches wide. The road passes through a range of habitats, including mountaintops and expansive basins where there is a good chance you will see plenty of desert wildlife. If you take the western side of the loop, you should plan ahead as it is very remote. On that section of the trail you may want to bring extra gas, water, and food with you.

The trail consists of a variety of different road types; everything from dirt and gravel to rocky areas with shelf ledges, to sand. The great thing about this trail is that you can take the easy route or take much harder sections.

While you are in the area, you should definitely visit the little town of Pioche. Oddly, it is considered both the county seat for Lincoln County and a ghost town. People still live and work there in Pioche, but there are sections that are truly part of the old ghost town. This old town has a very colorful past. Get this, the old mining town was so ruthless that its first 72 deaths were all murders. It even has a fairly large boothill cemetery to mark both the killers and many of their victims. Despite its colorful and deadly past, Pioche is now known as Nevada's liveliest ghost town.

Directions to Trailhead: Head southwest on US-93 S/Front St for 16.6 miles. Then turn north (right) onto N Poleline Rd.

Here is the QR code that shows all the major trails in this system:

Avenza Maps provides a great map of the entire trail and many of the side trails. The Nevada OHV website also has a great map to download. Sections of these trails can also be found on these apps: OnX Offroad, AllTrails+, and Trails Offroad.

## A Few Last Thoughts About Off-Roading in Nevada

There's no place quite like Nevada when it comes to exploring the great outdoors and pushing the limits of your off-road vehicle. With an abundance of public land, you'll have plenty of opportunities to embrace your adventurous spirit and tackle the hundreds of thrilling off-road trails.

Here is a website for more of Nevada's OHV trails:

Exploring these vast and exciting trail systems that span

across the state, off-roaders from all over the West flock to enjoy Nevada's expansive and unrestricted terrain. Get ready for some adrenaline-pumping adventures as you take on Nevada's diverse off-road and ATV trails. From challenging mountain roads to thrilling sand dunes, there's something for everyone. It's time to fasten that five-point harness and let the excitement begin!

# Chapter 9:

# Finding the Best Trails and Trail Systems in New Mexico

New Mexico offers plenty of wide-open spaces for some of the best off-roading adventures. With the right rig, you can explore various spaces, from off-roading day trips on designated trails to self-supported overnight travel on back roads.

### New Mexico OHV Permit Rules

There are hundreds of off-roading trails to explore in New Mexico, it is definitely a state you need to have on your bucket list. Thanks to the vast desert expanses and long stretches of sparsely populated land, discovering off-highway trails in this state is surprisingly simple.

### Robledo Mountains Trails System - Las Cruces, NM

Trail Rating: Moderately Easy 3 up to Extremely Difficult 9

Trail Type: Varies

Trail Length: Varies

Approximate Time: Varies

Best Season: Year Round

Traffic: Moderate

Trailhead Coordinates:  32.373371, -106.866832

All the trails in this area use the same parking area.  Use this QR code for all of them.

If you want to challenge yourself, then you should explore the Robledo Mountains OHV Trail System for some amazing trails. It has a network of trails has something for everyone, but specifically caters to extreme OHV enthusiasts in the scenic southern Robledo Mountains. The trails in the System are located within both the Prehistoric Trackways National Monument and the Organ Mountains-Desert Peaks National Monument.

Most of the trails are marked to inform drivers of the trail's rating (1-10). However, the vast majority of the trails located in the Robledo Mountain OHV system are rated moderate up to extremely difficult.

Many of the trails are filled with massive rocks, creating a very challenging terrain for riders. For those seeking adventure on the extreme OHV trails, with specialized vehicles with locking differentials, winches, and expert drivers are a must. Vehicle damage can occur on these challenging OHV trails.

This location is accessible all year without any charges.  You can find all the trails that are available on this trail system on the *Las Cruces Four Wheel Drive Club website under Robledo Mountain*.

Directions to Trailhead: From El Paso travel northbound on I-25 past the Las Cruces cloverleaf.  Take exit 9 for NM-320 toward Doña Ana, then turn left onto NM-320 W/Thorpe Rd. Turn right onto NM-185 N, and then left onto Shalem Colony Trail. Turn right onto Rocky Acres Trail,  then a slight left at the fork in the road onto a dirt road known as Permian Tracks Rd. Robledo Mountains OHV Staging Area is about a quarter of a mile up Permian Tracks Rd on your left.

**One thing that is cool about this area is that you can access almost all of the trails from the main Robledo Chili Canyons Loop.**

**Robledo Chili Canyons Loop**

Trail Rating: Moderate 4

Trail Type: Loop

Trail Length: 11 Miles

Approximate Time: 2-3 Hours

Best Season: Year Round

Traffic: Moderate

Trailhead Coordinates:  32.373371, -106.866832

Starting at the Robledo Mountains OHV Staging Area, this loop offers a nice balance of different terrains. Half of the trail can be completed in 2WD/4 High. The other half will need 4WD High/Low Range. The entire loop can be traversed by a driver with minimal off-road experience in a stock SUV that has high clearance and 4-low capability. There are no major obstacles, but some areas will require the driver's full attention.

This trail can be found on the Trails Offroad, OnX Offroad, and AllTrails apps, and at the Las Cruces Four Wheel Drive Club website under Robledo Mountain.

**Here is QR code with all 18 trails:**

Here are three of the eighteen great trails in the area that spur off from the main Robledo Loop.

- **Presidential Staircase**

**Trail Rating: Moderate 4**

Trail Type: Straight Through

Trail Length: 3/4 Mile

Approximate Time: 45 Minutes

Best Season: Year Round

Traffic: Moderate

Starting at the Robledo Mountains OHV Staging Area, this trail climbs around 400 feet, and is both rough and rocky. The steepest part is the Staircase the climb up several loose but shallow rocky steps. There will be some modestly off-camber parts and some loose patches across the primarily hard-packed dirt and rock trail surface. It is advised to have high clearance and 4WD on this trail. Any driver using this kind of vehicle should be able to handle this trail.

This trail can be found on the Trails Offroad app, and at the Las Cruces Four Wheel Drive Club website under Robledo Mountain.

- **Bell Pepper**

## Trail Rating: Moderately Difficult 6

Trail Type: Straight Through

Trail Length: 3/4 Mile

Approximate Time: 45 Minutes

Best Season: Year Round

Traffic: Moderate

This trail can be reached from the Robledo Mountains OHV Staging Area. Bell Pepper's terrain is divided into areas with solid rock slabs, loose rock, and hard-packed dirt and rock. A few portions are narrow, while others have a slight off-camber. This is a path best suited for drivers with some prior off-camber driving experience and a minimal amount of up-and-down vertical stepping. It is also helpful to have a lifted 4x4 with bigger tires.

This trail can also be found on the Trails Offroad app, and also at the Las Cruces Four Wheel Drive Club website under Robledo Mountain.

- **Rocotillo Rapids**

    Trail Rating: Extremely Difficult 9-10

    Trail Type: Straight Through

    Trail Length: 1.6 Miles

    Approximate Time: 3-4 hours

    Best Season: Year Round

    Traffic: Moderate

Starting at the Robledo Mountains OHV Staging Area. Practically all of the rocky trail on this straight-through crawl trail consists of both small and large boulders, and over-6-foot ledges. Only very capable vehicles driven by seasoned drivers should attempt this trail. Winching is probably the case with less-modified cars. Do not try this trail unless you are an expert driver with a good spotter. One seasoned driver summed this challenging route when he said, "It was hell, but I loved it."

This trail can be found on the Trails Offroad app, and also at the Las Cruces Four Wheel Drive Club website under Robledo Mountain.

Here is a brief overview of the other 16 amazing trails found in this system (from easy to hardest). All the trails can be accessed from the Robledo Mountains OHV Staging Area. **Here is a QR Code that provides a interactive map to all the trails:**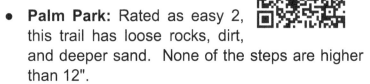

- **Palm Park:** Rated as easy 2, this trail has loose rocks, dirt, and deeper sand. None of the steps are higher than 12".

- **PTNM Entrance Rd:** Rated as easy 2, this trail has loose rocks, dirt, and deeper sand. None of the steps are higher than 12".

- **Palm Park:** Rated as moderately easy 3, this trail has loose rocks, dirt, sand with some easy slickrock surfaces. None of the steps are higher than 12".

- **Permian Reef Road:** Rated as moderately easy 3, this trail has loose rocks, dirt, sand with some fairly easy slickrock surfaces. None of the steps are higher than 12".

- **Acacia Ridge:** Rated as moderately easy 3, this trail has loose rocks, dirt, sand with some easy slickrock surfaces.

- **Pasado/Branson Overlook:** Rated as moderately easy 3, this trail has loose rocks, dirt, sand with some slickrock surfaces.

- **Chile Canyons Loop:** Rated as moderate 4, this trail has loose rocks, dirt, deep sand with some slickrock surfaces. No step ledges higher than 12".

- **PTNM Loop:** Rated as moderate 4, this trail has loose rocks, dirt, deep sand with some slickrock surfaces. No step ledges higher than 12".

- **Apache Canyon Access South:** Rated as moderate 4, this trail has loose rocks, dirt, deep sand with some slickrock surfaces. No step ledges higher than 12".

- **Amatista Ledges:** Rated as moderate 5, this trail has boulders up to 24", with ledge drops up to 3'.

- **Apache Canyon North:** Rated as moderate 5, this trail has loose rocks, dirt, and sand with some slickrock surfaces. None of the steps are higher than 12".

- **West Monument Boundary Road:** Rated as

moderate 5, this trail has boulders up to 12", with ledge drops less than 18".

- **Sandia Gulch:** Rated as Moderately Hard 7, this trail has boulders up to 20", with ledge drops up to 3'.

- **Amatista West Branch:** Rated as Hard 8, this trail has boulders up to 24", with ledge drops up to 3'.

- **Hopping Jalapeno:** Rated as Hard 8, this trail has boulders up to 24", with ledge drops up to 3'.

- **Big Jim:** Rated as Hard 8, this trail has boulders up to 24", with ledge drops up to 4'.

- **Habanero Falls:** Rated as Extremely Hard 10, this trail has boulders up to 36", with ledge drops up to 6'. VERY DANGEROUS.

## Red River - Taos, NM

There are a number of reasons why New Mexico is affectionately known as "The Land of Enchantment," and you'll understand why after seeing the Enchanted Circle. The Enchanted Circle is an 84-mile scenic byway that encircles Wheeler Peak and highlights the best aspects of New Mexico's distinctive history and scenic surroundings.

Off-roading through these beautiful mountains, aspen groves, ghost towns, and historic gold mines that surround Red River is an experience every outdoorsperson must experience to off-roading nirvana. For the ultimate Red River off-road adventure take your Jeep, or OHV on one (if not all) of the phenomenal roads or trails that the area has to offer.

Whether you are looking for beginner roads or demanding off-roading trails, the Red River's terrain will provide you with a lifetime of memories. Here are three great trails to consider:

- **Forest Service Road 376 - Jemez Springs, NM**

Trail Rating: Easy 1

Trail Type: Straight Through

Trail Length:  24 Miles

Approximate Time: 1-2 hours

Best Season:  Summer - Fall (Closed Winters)

Traffic: Moderate

Trailhead Coordinates: 35.668383, -106.743110

Wheeling on Forest Road 376 in the Santa Fe National Forest is a terrific way to see the best mountain beauty that New Mexico has to offer. This trail is a spur off from the iconic Jemez Mountain Trail, which is one of the most beautiful byways that you will ever drive.  The beginning of this scenic drive begins on pavement, but eventually becomes hardpack dirt and gravel.  Any motorcycle, car, SUV, or truck can easily travel this road.

Directions to Trailhead: From Jemez Springs Post Office travel southwest on NM-4 for 7.5 miles. Turn right at NM-485 N. Eventually NM-485 N will be marked as Forest Road 376.

You can find more information, maps, and waypoints for Forest Road 376 on these apps; Trails Offroads, OnX Offroad, and Gaia GPS.

- **Red River Pass and Fourth of July Canyon OHV Route**

Trail Rating:  Moderately Difficult 6

Trail Type: Point To Point

Trail Length: 7 Miles

Approximate Time: 2 hours

Best Season: Summer - Fall

Traffic: Moderate - Heavy

Trailhead Coordinates: 36.69118, -105.38773

Located close to Red River, New Mexico, this trail is widely regarded as a fairly difficult path. It is a fairly popular off-road trail, and often gets busy on weekends and holidays. A full-sized Jeep or similar sized 4X4 may have some challenges since there are a few places where vegetation gets very close. In the spring, expect deep ruts and downed timber along the route. Most 4x4s should have no problem navigating the first portion of the road to Red River Pass. The trail's difficulty levels range from moderate to hard, with the steeper parts being on the back side of the trail.

This picturesque trail also has optional obstacles along the way for those who are more adventurous. You can definitely put your vehicle through its paces in this off-road playground.

Directions to trailhead: From the Red River Post Office travel south on Main Street/NM-578 for 1.7 miles. On the left side of the road is the turnoff to Forest Access Road 488. As you exit NM-578 you will see a green street sign stating "Red River Pass, High Clearance Vehicles Only."

This trail can be found on both AllTrails+, OnX Offroads, Avenza, and Gaia GPS.

- **Goose Lake OHV Trail (FR 486)**

Trail Rating: Moderate 5

Trail Type: Out and Back

Trail Length: 14 miles

Approximate Time: 3+ hours

Best Season: Spring, Summer, Fall

Traffic: moderate

Trailhead Coordinates: 36.696683, -105.392574

This out-and-back trail is considered a moderately challenging route mainly because of the first couple of miles. This section requires good ground clearance and 4-low to deal with the nearly 2 ft deep water crossing and steep rocky terrain. This section of the road is a little sketchy for inexperienced drivers because of the narrow shelf roads. That being said, full size stock SUVs & trucks are still fine on this trail as long as you are a good driver.

The trail is fantastic for anyone who is willing to tackle it. The area around Goose Lake is stunning and definitely worth the journey! Expect to come across other off-road enthusiasts or fishers while exploring this road since it is a fairly popular drive to a beautiful lake.

Directions to Trailhead: From the Red River Post Office travel south on Main

Street/NM-578 for 1.2 miles. On the right side of the road is the turnoff for "Goose

Lake Rd" (aka Goose Lake Trail 66/FR 486).

You can find this road on most apps, including AllTrails+, OnX Offroad, Trails Offroads, Trailforks, Gaia GPS, and The Outbound.

## Caja del Rio OHV Trail (FR-24) - Santa Fe, NM

Trail Rating: Moderate 5

Trail Type: Loop

Trail Length: 21 Miles

Approximate Time: 3-4 hours

Best Season: Year around

Traffic: Low - Moderate

Trailhead Coordinates: 35.68965, -106.09213

This scenic 4x4 drive is fun and not too difficult. Most of the time, the area is dry and fun in March. If it rains,it can be messy and harder, however after a rain it is nice because the dust is low.

It is important to have a high clearance vehicle, and some parts of the trail may also require 4-low. Keep an eye out for wild horses that roam the area. If you have time to look around, there are several off-shoots on this trail to explore.

Directions to Trailhead: From Santa Fe, travel southwest on NM-599 S, then take exit 6 toward S Meadows Rd. At the traffic circle, take the 2nd exit onto NM-599 Frontage Rd for 1.4 miles. Then turn right onto Caja Del Rio Rd for 2.7 miles. Turn left at the sign that reads, "El Camino Real USFS Trailhead" onto County Rd 62 for 1.4 until you cross a cattle-guard. At the first fork in the road, veer right onto FR-24.

This trail can be found on Trailforks, AllTrails+, and OnX Offroad apps. You can also find maps of the area on the Forest Service website for the area, the local BLM office, or the 4X4 trail maps website.

## Elk Mountain - Tererro, NM

Trail Rating: Easy 2.5

Trail Type: Out and Back

Trail Length: 28 Miles

Approximate Time: 1-1.5 hours

Best Season: Spring - Fall

Traffic: Low

Trailhead Coordinates: 35.75101, -105.67204

This ride is fairly easy and has beautiful views all the way to the top. At 11,600 feet high, it is one of the highest roads in New Mexico.

There is a cow gate near the top that needs to be closed behind you. The trail gets rough and rocky after the gate. This is an excellent off-road trail for less experienced drivers, and is a beautifully easy drive for more experienced riders.

Remember that this is a mixed-use trail, so you can see bikers, hikers, and dog walkers throughout the route. However, it is likely that you won't run across many other visitors while exploring.

Directions to trailhead: From the north end of Tererro, head northwest on NM-63 toward Guadalupe Ln for 13 miles. Then turn right onto Forest Rd 646.

You can find this road on most apps, including AllTrails+, OnX Offroad, Trails Offroads, Trailforks, and Gaia GPS.

## Chokecherry Canyon/Glade Run Recreation Area (aka the Glade) - Farmington, NW

Trail Rating: Easy 1 to Most Difficult 10

Trail Type: Varies

Trail Length: Varies

Approximate Time: Varies

Best Season: Year Around

Traffic: Moderate to High

Trailhead Coordinates: 36.789340, -108.191127

More than one hundred different trails can be found within this amazing recreation area. There are 19,000 acres of open public property that make up the Glade Run Recreation Area, which is commonly referred to as the Glade. This area is located along the north and northwest side of Farmington. This well-known recreation area features a variety of terrains, including sandy arroyos, slick rock, rolling foothills, and mountain trails. There are paths available for UTVs, Jeeps, motorcycles, mountain bikes, and ATVs in the Glade. The location is accessible throughout the year, and dry overnight camping is permitted.

The Chokecherry Canyon trail system provides one of the most diverse trail systems found anywhere. Most of the trails range from moderate to difficult. If you want extremes, they have several trails listed as extremely difficult (9-10).

This playground in the high desert goes above and beyond expectations, including activities such as rock crawling, off-road tracks, and wash runs.

Directions to Main Trailhead: This area has several access locations via dirt roads and is situated between NM State Highways 170, 574, and 516. The Glade Road and Pinon Hills Boulevard crossroads is the simplest place to get to from Farmington. Trails can also be accessed from Hood Mesa, which is located north of the Farmington BLM field office at the end of College Boulevard.

Many of the trails have their own entry points. To get coordinates for each of the main 30 main trailheads in this area, follow this QR code:

ATV Pass - Socorro, NM

Trail Rating: Moderate 5

Trail Type: Straight Through

Trail Length: 2 miles

Approximate Time: 2 hours

Best Season: Year Around

Traffic: Low

Trailhead Coordinates: 34.126953, -106.805994

To get to Coyote Canyon you will need to travel up the Quebradas Backcountry Byway, then turn left on the Flagstone Road, then left again on the Overlook Road. You will then turn right into Coyote Canyon. We will then come out at the ATV Pass.

The trail offers an exciting drive with beautiful views and a sense of privacy. Aside from the stunning exposed geological features and picturesque landscapes in Coyote Canyon, there are numerous nearby offroading opportunities at different levels of technical challenge, creating a haven for 4WD enthusiasts. Sliders are recommended for tackling Coyote Canyon's steep shelf area.

Quebradas Backcountry Byway to Flagstone Road is an easy 2-3, ATV Pass is Moderate 5 which connects to Coyote Canyon Difficult 7.

Directions to Trailhead: From I-25: Take Escondida's Exit 152, travel east, and then bear north on the east frontage road for slightly over a mile to reach Escondida Lake. After crossing the Rio Grande River to the east, turn right at the Escondida Lake sign. Turn right at the T-intersection in Pueblito and proceed south approximately 1 mile to the start of the County Road A-152, often known as the Quebradas Backcountry Byway. To reach the trailhead on the left (north) side of the Byway, turn left (east) onto the Byway and proceed for 3.5 miles. Go one mile north to the T-intersection at the end of Flagstone Road. Start the ATV Pass trek by turning right (east).

The best app to get the full route is the TrailsOffroad app.

## A few final notes about New Mexico

New Mexico provides both novice and seasoned 4x4 riders with a delightful taste of the 4x4 lifestyle, with extremes from the nationally rated Chokecherry Canyon to the Robledo Mountains Trails System. This state has something for  everyone. We can guarantee a fun time when riding in New Mexico.

# Chapter 8:

# Finding the Best Trails and Trail Systems in Utah

Utah is the perfect destination for those who love extreme off-road adventures, boasting some of the most exciting off-roading trails in the United States. Obviously, it isn't the sole state with fantastic off-roading options. Many US states provide fantastic trails for those who enjoy exploring off-road paths, but Utah is still a popular choice due to its beautiful natural landscape and historic mining trails that provide not only exciting adventures but also fascinating tales.

For those who enjoy off-roading, the thrill lies in exploring new paths and embracing the journey rather than the final destination. Exploring the natural beauty and rocky formations, along with discovering pieces of human history, creates an unforgettable and enriching trip.

Much of Utah's landscape is inaccessible to those driving sedans and other street vehicles, but with the right off-road machine, you can enjoy it all. One can find everything from desert, to slickrock, to giant sand dunes, to mountain terrain, Utah is famous for its numerous scenic and challenging off-road trails. Let's take a look at some of the best trails available for 4X4s, side-by-sides, and ATVs for a thrilling ride.

## Utah OHV Permit Rules

When driven or carried on public roads or lands, all OHVs must have a current OHV registration sticker visible. Off-road bikes can be registered as street legal as long as they have been safety checked and are insured. OHV plates run out every year on the last day of the month the vehicle was bought.

People younger than 18 must have a youth OHV education license in order to ride an OHV on public land, a road, or a trail. People who are at least 18 years old and have a valid adult OHV education license can drive an OHV.

All registered cars, like jeeps, trucks, and more, don't need any extra permits.

## Slick Rock OHV Area - Moab, UT

Trail Rating: Moderately Easy 3 up to Extremely Difficult 9

Trail Type: Varies

Trail Length: Varies

Approximate Time: Varies

Best Season: Year Round

Traffic: Moderate

Trailhead Coordinates: 38.575360, -109.522870

The Moab Slickrock region is a destination that will never be forgotten because of its natural beauty, rich history, and hundreds of miles of abandoned mining roads and 4-wheel drive trails. Bring your own car, rent a jeep, or go on a trip with one of Moab's licensed and qualified guides. Never forget that you can only go on officially recognized motorized routes.

With a wide variety of backcountry trails ranging from easy scenic drives to the most difficult 4-wheel drive trails found anywhere, Moab offers everyone the chance to enjoy the peace and beauty of a backcountry adventure.

Directions to trailhead: From Moab Tourist Information Center head east on E Center St toward S 100 E/S 1st E St for 4/10s fo a mile. Turn right onto S 400 E/Fourth E St for nearly ½ miles, then just south of Milt's Stop and Eat, turn left onto S Mill Creek Dr for ½ mile. Continue to the fork in the road, stay left onto Sand Flats Rd. After the entrance station, there are multiple trailhead parking lots depending on what trail you are planning to use. The Sand Flats Recreation Area does charge an one time admission of $10 for a 7-day pass for all motorized vehicles except motorcycles.. Bikes or motorcycles have a lower entry fee of $5 for 7 days. The pass covers both Fins and Things & Hell's Revenge. None of the other trails in the area had any fees associated with them.

Here are my favorite trails found in the Moab Slickrock area.

- **Fins and Things - Sand Flats Recreation Area, Moab, UT**

  Trail Rating: Moderate 5

  Trail Type: Point To Point

  Trail Length: 9 Miles

  Approximate Time: 4 Hours

  Best Season: Year Around

  Traffic: Moderate - High

  Trailhead Coordinates: 38.582558, -109.503120

Exploring the vast expanse of slickrock domes in the Sand Flats Recreation Area, just a few miles east of the town of Moab, this amazingly fun ONE-WAY trail awaits. It is famous as a Jeep Badge Of Honor Trail, which provides a moderately hard trail with spacious access routes between each obstacle, allowing for easier bypasses for the less experienced driver and several exit points.

151

This trail consists of sand, loose rock, dirt, and plenty of Slickrock surfaces. Expect to find washes, ravines, and rock steps no higher than 18 inches. Tall tires (32 inches or greater) and lockers are a plus. Having 4WD is required. Having enhanced suspension and good ground clearance are helpful. Good driving skills are also a plus. Stock Jeeps and other SUVs with skid protection, and a good driver should be able to handle the easier version of this route.

Directions to trailhead: From Moab Tourist Information Center head east on E Center St toward S 100 E/S 1st E St for 4/10s for a mile. Turn right onto S 400 E/Fourth E St for nearly ½ miles, then just south of Milt's Stop and Eat, turn left onto S Mill Creek Dr for ½ mile. Continue to the fork in the road, stay left onto Sand Flats Rd. After the entrance station, turn into the first parking lot on your left.

You will get a map at the entrance station, which shows all of the trails in the recreation area. You can find this trail on the following apps: Alltrails+, OnX Offroad, Trails Offroad, Gaia GPS, and Avenza Maps.

This is one of my favorite trails, and I always have to take it in Moab.

- **Hell's Revenge - Sand Flats Recreation Area, Moab, UT**

Trail Rating: Moderately Hard 6

Trail Type: Loop

Trail Length: 8 Miles

Approximate Time: 4 Hours

Best Season: Year Around

Traffic: Moderate-High

Trailhead Coordinates: 38.575360, -109.522870

For many wheelers, Moab's Hell's Revenge is an absolute must-do. Also known as a Jeep Badge Of Honor Trail, this premier trail provides a variety of challenges, including steep climbs, descents, and some edges that are not for the faint of heart. Due to hazardous conditions, experienced riders are recommended for this trail. These challenges, along with the stunning scenery, create a truly fulfilling adventure.

You'll find the trailhead just beyond the entrance station. Exploring sand and a slickrock rollercoaster, thrilling climbs on fins, steep ascents and descents, sharp turns, and insane traction issues, Hells Revenge promises an exciting ride at every corner.

It is recommended that a spotter be used on tricky sections. Drivers should also have the appropriate equipment, such as 33-inch tires, a lift, a winch, and lockers.

Directions to trailhead: From Moab Tourist Information Center head east on E Center St toward S 100 E/S 1st E St for 4/10s fo a mile. Turn right onto S 400 E/Fourth E St for nearly ½ miles, then just south of Milt's Stop and Eat, turn left onto S Mill Creek Dr for ½ mile. Continue to the fork in the road, stay left onto Sand Flats Rd. After the entrance station, Turn left onto Sand Flats Rd for 1.6 miles. You will see a sign on the right showing the Fins and Things trailhead. If you are pulling a trailer, the best places to park a trailer are at either the Hell's Revenge parking lot, or the Slickrock Bike Trail parking lot.

You can find this trail on the following apps; Alltrails+, OnX Offroad, Trails Offroad, Gaia GPS, and Avenza Maps.

- **Poison Spider Mesa - Moab, UT**

  Trail Rating: Moderate 6 Difficult 8

  Trail Type: Out and Back Loop

  Trail Length: 13.5 Miles

  Approximate Time: 5 - 6 Hours

  Best Season: Year Round

  Traffic: Moderate - Heavy

  Trailhead Coordinates: 38.532633, -109.608773

This trail is a favorite among many who off-road in this area of Utah. Exploring Poison Spider Mesa offers an exciting mix of thrilling challenges combined with breathtaking views. This trail in Moab is a favorite among many and is frequently paired with Golden Spike and Gold Bar Rim. Check out the amazing Little Arch near the cliff edge with a view of Moab. It's important to remember that mountain bikers often use this road. It is a challenging ride, and so it is sometimes easy to forget that bikers are also on this trail.

Keep in mind that this route is rated as moderate to difficult because it can be challenging, with large ledges and unstable areas. This is best suited for customized vehicles with high ground clearance, lockers, oversized tires, and excellent articulation. Finding your way on the loop section of the trail can be quite tricky. Enjoy following the track and admiring the painted Jeep symbols.

This trail offers a variety of terrain challenges, including slick rock, deep sand, dry waterfalls, steep ledges, and hill climbs. While many of the harder obstacles can be avoided with bypass options, some are mandatory for the trail. Anticipate 6-foot tall waterfalls, steeper than 30-degree inclines, and numerous drops that will likely drag your bumper. For those who enjoy a thrilling off-road adventure, your vehicle should be modified with a lift, larger tires, and lockers.

By taking the bypasses rather than the optional extreme sections, this trail is manageable in a stock Jeep or SUV with an experienced driver and careful tire placement, but you should definitely be prepared for some undercarriage scraping.

Directions to Trailhead: From Moab Center St head north on US-191 N/N Main St for 4 miles. Turn left onto UT-279/Potash Rd for 5.9 miles. On your right you will see a sign and parking lot for the Poison Spider Trailhead.

You can find this trail on the following apps; Alltrails+, OnX Offroad, Trails Offroad, Gaia GPS, and Avenza Maps.

- **Metal Masher - Moab, UT**

  Trail Rating: Difficult 7

  Trail Type: Straight Through

  Trail Length: 12 Miles

  Approximate Time: 4-5 Hours

  Best Season: Year Round

  Traffic: Moderate

  Trailhead Coordinates: 38.59642, -109.69373

Metal Masher is approximately named for all the scars it has left on vehicles that take it on. The trail begins and ends as an easy, sandy road, but the terrain changes into a large slickrock area with towering cliffs. There are dozens of step ledges and switchbacks, dried waterfalls, slopes greater than 30 degrees, and drops that will drag your tail if you aren't sufficiently lifted.

It is recommended to have a modified vehicle with high

ground clearance, lockers, large tires, and a winch before taking on this trail. Fortunately, the trail is well-marked so it is easy to follow. Many of the hardest challenges (aptly named Mirror Gulch, Rock Chucker, and yes--Widow Maker) have bypass routes for the less experienced drivers, but there are still plenty of hurdles that everyone has to traverse.

Directions to Trailhead: From Moab Center St head north on US-191 N/N Main St, continue north for 9.7 miles on Hwy 191 and turn left onto the Gemini Bridges road. Immediately turn again to stay on Gemini Bridges Rd. Follow the Gemini Bridges road for 6 miles, turning north (right) onto the Metal Masher Trailhead. There are signposts along the way.

You can find this trail on the following apps; Alltrails+, OnX Offroad, Trails Offroad, Gaia GPS, and Avenza Maps.

## Arapeen Trail System - Manti, UT

Trail Rating:  Easy 2 - Hard 7

Trail Type: Varies

Trail Length: Varies

Approximate Time:  Varies

Best Season: Summer - Fall

Traffic: Low - Moderate

**To get the individual maps for all the trails along Arapeen Trail use this QR Code:**

The famed Aapreen Trail system has the nickname "Side-by-Side Heaven." It is truly an off-road enthusiast's dream come true. This adventure hub spans 350,000 acres of pristine National Forest and features over 600 miles of friendly side-by-side routes. While you wander through this beautiful, serene expanse, you'll be enveloped by stunning Aspen and Pine forests with trout-filled mountain lakes that provide truly stunning scenic views.

There are plenty of areas for the whole family to play in, as well as many advanced trails for experienced riders. For street-legal vehicles all you need is a driver's license. OHVs need a UT OHV Sticker.

Note that the trails within the Aapreen Trail system are made up of several forest roads chained together. There are seven canyons in the Sanpete Valley that provide access to this vast trail system. These valleys include the towns of Fairview, Ephraim, and Manti.

**Below are four of the twenty-plus amazing trails that can be found at this OHV system:**

- **Skyline Drive #1 - Ephraim, UT**

    Trail Rating: Easy 2-3

    Trail Type: Point to point

    Trail Length: 74 Miles

    Approximate Time: 9 hours

    Traffic: Moderate

    Northern Trailhead Coordinates: 39.935836, -111.200008

    There are seven canyons in the Sanpete Valley that provide access to this vast trail. These valleys include the towns of Fairview, Ephraim, and Manti.

    Skyline trail #1 of the Arapeen ATV Trail System runs from Highway 6 (between mile markers 203 & 204) the drive goes south and finishes at I-70 near Redmond, Utah. It picks up again on the far side of I-70 and continues south to Torrey, UT. Most of the time, the road is in good shape, and you can pull a trailer on much of it. On the road, there are a lot of rustic camping spots.

What's the best part? Because all the Arepeen trails link with the towns below, you can ride up one canyon, check out a portion of the "Skyline" at the top of the mountain, and then go back down to another town through a different canyon. This is the perfect place to enjoy the peace and quiet of this secret gem by getting lost in nature. It's time to get your Jeep/Truck/OHV/ATV ready, and hit the road for a trip like no other.

Directions to the northern trailhead:  From Spanish Fork, UT take US-6 eastbound into Spanish Fork Canyon for 28.7 miles.  Turn Right at the sign that reads "Skyline Drive."

## Fred's Flat Loop - Ephraim, UT

Trail Rating: Moderate 5

Trail Type: Loop

Trail Length:  17 Miles

Approximate Time: 3 hours

Traffic: Low

Trailhead Coordinates:  39.340351, -111.539718

This fun OHV loop that heads up New Canyon, cuts across Fred's Flat and Left-Land

Fork road, and then returns to Ephraim on the Main Canyon road. In June and early July, there is a deep creek crossing.    Beyond that, be prepared for off-camber sections and rocky areas with some ledges.

Directions to trailhead:  From Ephraim, turn left onto E 400 S. Turn south (right) onto 300 East for .6 mile and then turn east (left) onto Ephraim Canyon Rd for 2.2 miles.  Fred's Flat Loop begins and ends when the two roads,  FR 3900 and Ephraim Canyon Rd (FR 0008) meet.

## Hanging Tree 4×4 Route

Trail Rating: Difficult 9-10

Trail Type: Out and Back

Trail Length:  3 Miles

Approximate Time: 3 hours

Traffic: Low

Trailhead Coordinates: 39.369593, -111.696074

This trail is for those who enjoy a challenge and have advanced 4×4 driving skills because of extreme 4WD rock crawling. Front and rear lockers, oversized tires with rugged tread, and a winch are strongly advised, along with spare parts and a support team. This trail offers a variety of terrain, including rocks, steps, waterfalls, and mud.  There is a risk of vehicle damage and personal injury. Proceed with great care!

The Hanging Tree Trail starts on Public Land (BLM), but the area at the top of the trail is privately owned. It is important to refrain from littering or damaging the property and make sure that you close the gates behind you.

Directions to trailhead: From Ephraim Main St/Hwy 89 travel westbound on 100 North to 1000 E.  Turn right through the curve on 1000 East the Ephraim River Ln. and then veer left and continue on the River Lane for 2.5 miles.  Then turn right onto River Lane Rd.  Then stay left on Dry Canyon road for .7 mile where you will find a parking loop area.

## Log Maple Canyon Loop - Fountain Green, UT

Trail Rating:  Moderately Easy 3

Trail Type: Loop

Trail Length: 28 Miles

Approximate Time: 3 hours

Best Season: Summer-Fall

Traffic: Low

Trailhead Coordinates: 39.555429, -111.660836

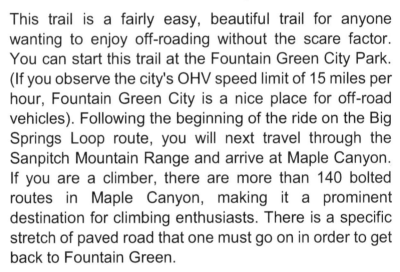

This trail is a fairly easy, beautiful trail for anyone wanting to enjoy off-roading without the scare factor. You can start this trail at the Fountain Green City Park. (If you observe the city's OHV speed limit of 15 miles per hour, Fountain Green City is a nice place for off-road vehicles). Following the beginning of the ride on the Big Springs Loop route, you will next travel through the Sanpitch Mountain Range and arrive at Maple Canyon. If you are a climber, there are more than 140 bolted routes in Maple Canyon, making it a prominent destination for climbing enthusiasts. There is a specific stretch of paved road that one must go on in order to get back to Fountain Green.

Directions to trailhead: From I-15 take Nephi exit 225. to Manti/Ephraim. Follow Hwy-132 to Fountain Green. You'll see a Maple Canyon sign when you toward the far end of town (400 S St). Freedom Road is 6 miles after turning right on 400-south. From here, follow the signs.

## Sand Hollow State Park - Hurricane, UT

Trail Rating: Easy 2 - Hard 9

Trail Type: Loops, Straight Through, and combinations

Trail Length: Varies

Approximate Time: Varies

Best Season: October - June

Traffic: Low - High

Trailhead Coordinates: 37.10294, -113.40415

Next to Moab, Sand Hollow is a new off-roading haven that's drawing in a wide range of off-road enthusiasts. Sand Hollow State Park is an absolute paradise for those who love adventure and appreciate the beauty of nature. It has become a popular destination for off-road enthusiasts and nature lovers alike. Less than 15 minutes from St George, Utah, this off-road system has something for everyone. Everything from slickrock challenges and major rock crawling, to giant rolling sand dunes, to easy scenic drives, this location has something for everyone.

Experience the thrill of exploring 62,000 acres of exhilarating trails and dunes. There are trails that are easy up to the most difficult and extreme obstacles anywhere. Why do you think the famed Matt's Off Road Recovery is based here? It's not just because he loves the climate (even though that is a great plus to this location).

The park requires all off-road vehicles to have an 8' flag. Most of the trails at Sand Hollow require 4WD with good all-terrain tires and good clearance.

Sand Hollow is open all year round, but can get very hot from June through August.

There are literally dozens of trails you can take in this area. The main trails can be found on most off-road apps, including; AllTrails+, OnX Offroad, Trails Offroad, Gaia GPS, Avenza, and Garmin maps.

Directions to Sand Hollow: Take the Hurricane (Exit 16) exit off of I-15. After around four miles of eastbound Hwy 9, turn right into Sand Hollow Road. After roughly three miles of traveling south, drive under the overpass (for the Southern Sand Hollow Parkway). The road will go from paved to dirt and about 100 yards further up the dirt road will be a large parking lot. This is the main trailhead for all the trails at Sand Hollow.

The Fee structure is $15 on Weekdays, $20* on Fridays and Sundays ($10 for those over 65).

$125 for an regular annual pass to all state parks with an annual Senior Pass set at $65.

**This is a QR code that provides a map for the entire Sand Hollow State Park and all of the trails:**

Here are four of the most popular trails found at Sand Hollow State Park:

- **West Rim Trail to Fault Line Trails**

  Trail Rating: Moderate 4 to Moderately Hard 6 (bypass options available)

  Trail Type: Loop

  Trail Length: 12.5 miles

  Approximate Time: 2 hours

  Best Season: October - early June

  Traffic: Low - moderate

  Typically seen as a route that offers a decent level of challenge. This trail is perfect for those who enjoy off-road driving and prefer a more secluded experience. It begins with a thrilling ascent up a steep red clay slope, leading to a rocky terrain. There are a few exciting ledges and climbs to conquer before reaching a challenging boulder. You'll need to navigate around the boulder with a thrilling off-camber curve, followed by an exhilarating 40 ft off-camber descent.

- **Milt's Mile Extended Loop Trail (parts 1 & 2 combined)**

Trail Rating: Moderate 4 to Hard 8 (bypass options available)

Trail Type: Loop

Trail Length: 4.5 miles

Approximate Time: 2 hours

Best Season: October - June

Traffic: Low - Moderate

Milt's Mile has to parts (#1 & 2) that connect into this 4.5 mile loop. This 4.5-mile loop is suitable for a variety of off-road vehicles and is generally considered a moderate ride. Parts of the trail are somewhat difficult however bypasses exist at all the difficult sections should you choose the easier route. This trail features off-camber twists, steep bowl climbs, stair-step ledges, and some difficult v-notches, among other continuous slickrock challenges. This well-liked trail offers a variety of obstacles and is a terrific drive for a variety of off-road vehicles, regardless of vehicle size, as long as you have 4WD and high clearance. Milt's Mile offers breathtaking vistas of Sand Hollow Reservoir, Zion National Park cliffs, Pine Valley Mountains, and colorful desert canyons and rock formations.

- **Wayne's World**

Trail Rating: Moderately Hard 6

Trail Type: Point to Point

Trail Length: 6 miles

Approximate Time: 4 hours

Best Season: October - June

Traffic: Moderate

Wayne's World is a fantastic trail that begins and ends

163

along the Highway 7 fence line trail on Sand Mountain. On this trail, you'll get to tackle a variety of exciting obstacles including sand dunes, slickrock, off-camber sections, washes, and ledges. The route offers breathtaking views of Zion National Park, The Pine Valley Mountains, the Hurricane Cliffs, and Sand Hollow Reservoir. It is a popular route because it offers such a variety of challenges.

- **Double Sammy**

  Trail Rating: Difficult 8

  Trail Type: Point to Point

  Trail Length: 1 miles

  Approximate Time: 2 hours

  Best Season: October - June

  Traffic: Low - Moderate

  This trail is mostly slickrock. From the very start of the trail, you immediately sense what the rest of the journey will be like–and that is a technically challenging ride. Double Sammy offers a wide variety of challenging terrain, including off-camber sections, steep climbs, shelves, and more. It's a trail that will keep you on your toes and provide plenty of excitement. This trail is an absolute blast, but having the right vehicle to enjoy it fully is important. Without the right tires, clearance, lockers on the vehicles, and an experienced driver behind the wheel, this trai experience might not be as exhilarating as it is scary.

# Little Sahara Recreation Area - Delta, UT

Trail Rating: Easy 2 - Hard 9

Trail Type: Loops, Straight Through, and combinations

Trail Length: Varies

Approximate Time: Varies

Best Season: September - May

Traffic: Low - High (depending on season & holidays)

Trailhead Coordinates: 39.726489, -112.307417

Located in the northwest corner of the expansive Sevier Desert, just a short drive west of I-15, lies the Little Sahara Recreation Area (LRSA).

Visiting this sand-dune locale is an absolute blast, thanks to its vast 60,000 acres of open riding area. You won't be disappointed! There's a wide variety of things to enjoy here. These expansive dunes are ideal for allowing beginners to practice and improve their skills. The massive bowls on the back of Sand Mountain are a thrilling attraction for those who love exhilarating roller-coaster-style rides. And yeah, what about that massive hill called Sand Mountain?! It's such a blast! This towering dune lives up to its name, offering a thrilling test of horsepower with its giant wall of sand standing nearly 700 feet tall. However, if you aren't up to a mountain of sand, there's no need to fret. This site provides magnificent rolling dunes with flowing bowls, big jumps, and open riding spaces with numerous desert trails for those who aren't ready to take on the mountain.

You should be aware that Little Sahara attracts a large number of visitors each year, especially during popular holiday weekends like Easter, Memorial Day, and Labor Day. If you're able to schedule your trip during other times, you'll have a much more enjoyable experience without the large crowds.

Coordinate to Little Sahara entrance: From Nephi, take Highway 132 and Juab County Road 1812 west for about 28 miles. Take Highway 6 north for about 38 miles from Delta. Take Highway 6 south for about 23 miles past Eureka. There is a fee for a two-day, one-night camping permit costs $18 per car and expires at sunset the second day. First car annual permit is $120, second vehicle $65. All Little Sahara costs are 50% off for seniors.

You can find maps about this area on Avenza maps, and also on the Little Sahara BLM website, or at the visitor center/entrance booth of the area.

## San Rafael Swell - Castledale, UT

Trail Rating: Moderately Easy 3 - 4

Trail Type: Point To Point

Trail Length: 33 Miles

Approximate Time: 6 Hours

Best Season:  Spring-Fall

Traffic: Low

Trailhead Coordinates: 39.16814, -110.75538

The San Rafael Swell is an amazing hidden gem nestled in the heart of Utah. This incredible landscape covers over 1,500 square miles and is renowned for its breathtaking canyons, striking rock formations, and fascinating ancient rock art. However, exploring "The Swell" can be a bit perplexing if you don't know the area!

Many of the routes throughout the San Rafael Swell area can be driven with any AWD or 4WD.  However some trails require more, so alway check before proceeding on a new trail.

Here are 3 trails in the San Rafael Swell that you will enjoy:

## San Rafael Swell Wedge Overlook - Castledale, UT

Trail Rating: Easy 2-3

Trail Type: Point To Point

Trail Length: 14 Miles

Approximate Time: 2 Hours

Best Season: Spring-Fall

Traffic: Low

Trailhead Coordinates: 39.175167, -110.790841

Wedge Coordinates: 39.16814, -110.75538

The Wedge is one of Utah's hidden gems, and well worth seeing. From the Wedge Overlook, you can see what is known as the Little Grand Canyon of the San Rafael River in a way that can't be beat. At either end of the Rim, there are two main places to park. The road and trail along the rim link the two parking lots, making it easy for people on foot and in cars.

The Wedge is an absolute delight to visit, it's a fantastic location that can easily fit into your itinerary, no matter what other activities you have planned in the area.

Directions to the Wedge: To get there, take Hwy. 10 south from Price. When you leave Hwy 10 about a mile north of Castle Dale, turn left (east) on the good, graveled Buckhorn Draw Road. Drive for 12.6 miles until you reach a signposted intersection with a small cinder block house called Buckhorn Well. For the mid-level ride to the lookout, turn right (south) and go for half a mile to the parking area. For those who are just starting out, take the left fork and go down Wedge Overlook Road for about 4 miles. At the next fork in the road, there is plenty of parking where you can begin your trail ride. For more experienced riders, the tour can start 11 miles further back on the main Buckhorn Draw Road.

## The Devil's Racetrack

Trail Rating: Moderately Hard 5-6

Trail Type: Point To Point

Trail Length: 17-34 Miles (depending on route choices)

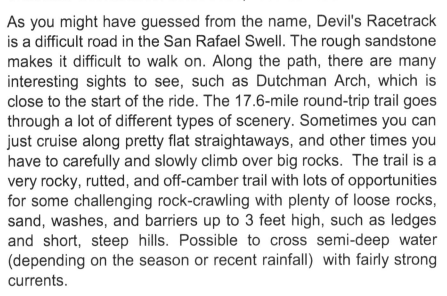

Approximate Time: 5 -7 Hours

Best Season:  Spring-Fall

Traffic: Low

Trailhead Coordinates: 38.893454, -110.651498

As you might have guessed from the name, Devil's Racetrack is a difficult road in the San Rafael Swell. The rough sandstone makes it difficult to walk on. Along the path, there are many interesting sights to see, such as Dutchman Arch, which is close to the start of the ride. The 17.6-mile round-trip trail goes through a lot of different types of scenery. Sometimes you can just cruise along pretty flat straightaways, and other times you have to carefully and slowly climb over big rocks.  The trail is a very rocky, rutted, and off-camber trail with lots of opportunities for some challenging rock-crawling with plenty of loose rocks, sand, washes, and barriers up to 3 feet high, such as ledges and short, steep hills. Possible to cross semi-deep water (depending on the season or recent rainfall)  with fairly strong currents.

There are beautiful views of Devil's Canyon, but there are also sights to see almost everywhere along the trail.

Directions to Trailhead:  From I-70 take exit 131 (Temple Mt Rd) heading north.  After exiting the freeway, immediately north of the freeway is a cattle guard.  Just past the cattle guard is a large dirt parking area to the left of the frontage road.

You can find variations of this trail on AllTrails+, OnX Offroad, Avenza Maps, Trails Offroad, and Trailforks.

## The North Fork, Fixit Pass, Cane Wash

**This 3 in one trail is a great ride:  North Fork, Fixit Pass, Cane Wash**

Trail Rating: Easy to Moderate 3-4

Trail Type: Point To Point

Trail Length: 33 Miles

Approximate Time: 6 Hours

Best Season:  Spring-Fall

Traffic: Low

Trailhead Coordinates:  39.04199, -110.92641

This combined route takes you through a variety of terrains found in the San Rafael Swell. Plus, this route also provides you with the opportunity to explore other well-known off-roading trails in the area. There is always beautiful scenery and a few challenges, so feel free to choose your own distance if you don't want to do the entire route.

Start at a spacious open lot located at the end of Horn Silver Gulch. Driving through the wash is quite an experience! The soft dirt allows for some exhilarating speeds, while also requiring careful crawling at times. One must not miss the incredible Swasey's Arch, a true gem of the area. Once you reach Fixit Pass, get ready for an exciting challenge as you navigate through a series of boulders, testing your clearance and wheel placement skills. The final section, Cane Wash, offers breathtaking scenery and intriguing remnants of past mining activity.

You will need a vehicle with good clearance to do the "Fix It Pass" section of the trail.

This route takes you through a variety of terrains in the San Rafael Swell, including North Fork Wash, Fixit Pass, and Cane Wash. It's a great adventure for those who love to explore!

Additionally, it grants you the opportunity to explore other well-known off-roading trails in the vicinity. There is always beautiful scenery and a few challenges, so feel free to choose your own distance if you don't want to complete the entire route. Start at a spacious open lot located at the end of Horn Silver Gulch. Driving through the wash is quite an experience, with the soft dirt allowing for some thrilling moments of higher speeds, while also requiring careful crawling at times. One must-see attraction is Swasey's Arch. Once you reach Fixit Pass, get ready for an exciting challenge as you navigate through a series of boulders that demand precise clearance and careful wheel placement. The final section is Cane Wash, which offers breathtaking scenery and intriguing remnants of old mining operations. There are plenty of opportunities for dispersed camping along the way.

Directions to trailhead: From Castle Dale travel South on UT-10 approximately 7.5 miles. Immediately after the village of Clawson, turn left onto S Maple Rd/Molen Cutoff. Travel 5.7 miles when the road turns into E Dutch Flt/FR705. After 9.9 miles E Dutch Flt/FR705 road will have a fork. E Dutch Flt/FR705 will go right and Dutch Flat Rd/FR3515 will go left. The staging area is at that fork in the road.

You can find more about this on Avenza Maps, Gaia GPS, Alltrails+, Trails Offroad, and OnX Offroad. Here is a link to this fun tour:

White Rim Trail - Moab, UT

Trail Rating: Easy to Moderate 2 - 4

Trail Type: Point To Point

Trail Length: 100 Miles

Approximate Time: 2 - 3 Days

Best Season: March - June, or Sept - November are best

Traffic: Low - Moderate

Trailhead coordinates from the top of Shafer Trail: 38.471567, -109.811496

This 100-mile White Rim Road offers a fantastic opportunity to explore the breathtaking views of the surrounding area as it loops around and below the Island in the Sky mesa top. Four-wheel-drive trips typically last for two to three days, while mountain bike trips usually span three to four days.

The White Rim Road offers a thrilling adventure for those seeking a bit of excitement behind the wheel. With favorable weather conditions, this route presents a moderate challenge for high-clearance, four-wheel-drive vehicles. The exhilarating sections of the Shafer Trail, Lathrop Canyon Road, Murphy Hogback, Hardscrabble Hill, and the Mineral Bottom switchbacks add an exciting element to the White Rim loop, making it a thrilling mountain bike ride. It's important to exercise caution when riding in inclement weather to ensure the safety of both vehicles, motorcycles, and bikes. ATVs & OHVs are not allowed on this trail.

I personally recommend starting at the top of the Shafer Trail and driving in a clockwise circle around the White Rim, culminating in a final ascent out of Mineral Bottom.

You need to get a day-use permit online the night before if your trip doesn't go by a visitor center or starts early (before regular business hours). If you are planning to stay overnight on the trail, be sure and plan ahead. In the spring and fall, there are often more people who want overnight permits than there are permits available. You should make bookings well in advance if you want to visit Canyonlands during these times.

Directions to the Trailhead: From Moab, Head north on US-191 N for 9 miles. At the Moab Giants Dinosaur Park, turn left onto UT-313 W for the next 15 miles. Past the Dead Horse Point

State Park exit and drave another 7.5 miles. There will be a sign to turn left for the Shafer Trail Road and White Rim.

## Last Thoughts About Off Roading In Utah

There are a number of off-roading trails in Utah that are considered to be among the best in the United States. Off-road fans flock to this state because of its varied topography, which includes both desert and mountainous terrain.

Because there are so many different types of off-highway trails available for every level of rider, you are sure to have a good time taking on some of the more than 80,000 miles of public off-highway vehicle trails found in Utah.

# Chapter 9:

# Finding the Best Trails and Trail Systems in Wyoming

If you're seeking an adventurous escape from the ordinary, Wyoming is an ideal destination to satisfy your craving for excitement. The state's diverse terrain offers a wide range of off-roading adventures, perfect for everyone, regardless of their skill level. From rolling plains to desert runs, sandy dunes, or rugged mountains, there's something for everyone to enjoy. Wyoming's trails cater to all levels of off-roaders, ensuring an enjoyable experience for everyone, regardless of your skill level.

In a nutshell, Wyoming has enough room to enjoy offroading to your heart's content. With all of this open space, it should come as no surprise that  Wyoming's great outdoors attracts people from within and outside the Intermountain West. Many off-roaders enjoy the wilderness trails of this great state. We have compiled a list of some of the most beautiful places in Wyoming that are ideal for off-roading for your consideration.

## Wyoming ORV (Off Road Vehicle) Permit Rules:

When driving on USFS, BLM, State Park, or other roads that are part of the Wyoming ORV Program, drivers must have a valid operator license and proof of liability insurance. The ORV must also have a current Wyoming ORV Permit and working brake lights, tail lights, and headlamps if it is being driven from half an hour after sunset to half an hour before sunrise.

## Morrison Jeep Trail - Cody, WY

Trail Rating: Moderately Difficult 7

Trail Type: Straight Through

Trail Length: 22 Miles

Approximate Time: 7 Hours

Best Season: Summer-Fall

Traffic: Low

Trailhead Coordinates: 44.846361, -109.314419

Right up front, you should be aware that this trail is very tough. It should only be run by an experienced driver in an adequate 4WD vehicle or OHV.  This trail is quite mentally challenging, leaving no room for error or second-guessing. To make it to the top of the trail, you can expect 27 tight switchbacks with no by-passes, it's a single track, very rocky, slippery, and dangerous road up the mountain gaining a lot of elevation all at once up steep grades. The turns are very narrow and steep, so you better have nerves of steel!

This trail is filled with rocks and boulders that keep your travel quite slow throughout.  Bringing long-wheelbase vehicles to this location is not recommended since they will have some problems working through the unyielding switchbacks.

There are not many options for winch points along the trail, and few, if any, turn around areas or room to pass along narrow shelf roads.

Lowering your tire pressure is a wise plan on this trail, and having plenty of patience not to rush this trail is important. It is recommended not to take this road alone.

Directions to trailhead: Travel 30 miles north on the Belfry Highway/Wyoming Highway 120 from Cody. Take Wyoming Highway 292 (Road 1Ab) to the left or northwest. After traveling 3.5 miles on Road 1Ab/Wyoming 292/Canyon Road, bear left at the split to stay on this route. Continue on it for a further 7.7 kilometers until you reach a large interpretative sign on your left. This is the south trailhead, and it's an excellent spot to park and let your trailer air out. Proceed south on MT-72 N from Bellfry, Montana; near the Wyoming border, this route becomes Belfry Highway/Wyoming Highway 120. Continue for 18.7 miles. Take Wyoming Highway 292 (Road 1Ab) to the right or northwest. After traveling 3.5 miles on Road 1Ab/Wyoming 292/Canyon Road, bear left at the split to stay on this route. Continue on it for a further 7.7 kilometers until you reach a large interpretative sign on your left. This is the south trailhead, and it's an excellent spot to park and let your trailer air out. It might be easier to get groups together before heading onto Road 1Ab, as you will probably lose cell coverage after that.

You can find more about this on Gaia GPS, AllTrails+, Avenza, OnX Offroad, and Trails Offroad.

## McCullough Peaks OHV area - Cody, WY

Trail Rating: Easy 2 - Moderately Hard 7

Trail Type: Varies

Trail Length:  Varies

Approximate Time:  Varies

Best Season: Summer - Fall

Traffic: Low

Trailhead Coordinates: 44.50590, -108.92796

McCullough Peaks offers a vast network of trails spanning over 150 miles, allowing you to enjoy a variety of terrains.  The landscape is full of sharp ridges and deeply eroded drainage areas, adding a touch of excitement to the surroundings–and to your ride.  The area is absolutely stunning and offers plenty of chances for peacefulness and unspoiled riding without running into many (if any) other travelers..

The breathtaking views from the top of McCullough Peaks are absolutely stunning, showcasing not only the area's badlands but also offering glimpses of Heart Mountain, the Beartooth Mountains, and the Absaroka Range.

There are plenty of exciting trails to enjoy in the area.   The vibrant hues and beautifully weathered ridges and hills possess an exceptional scenic allure.  Keep an eye out for wildlife, there are an abundance of deer, antelope, and yes even wild horses in the area.

Directions to trailhead: From Cody, Head southeast on US-14 E/US-16 E/US-20 E for 6 miles.  Turn left onto McCullough Peaks Rd.  The trailhead is on the right of the road.

There is no charge for riding in this vast area, but it is important to have a valid Wyoming ORV permit for all machines. All vehicles must have a spark arrestor exhaust silencer or end cap.

## Killpecker Sand Dunes - Rock Springs, WY

Trail Rating: East 1 to Hard 7

Trail Type: Sand dunes that range from 10' to 400' high

Trail Length: Over 11,000 acres of dune trails

Approximate Time:  As long as you can ride

Best Season: Spring - Fall

Traffic: Moderate to High

Trailhead Coordinates: 41.961549, -109.081160

Explore the stunning Killpecker Sand Dunes, where you'll find a fascinating display of nature's power. The dunes have become a popular destination for OHVs and ATVs, attracting motorsport enthusiasts from all over the country. Come and experience the thrill of exploring our vast 11,000 acres of open play space with your Jeep, dune buggy, dirt bike, ATV, or OHV! Beginner riders can start off on more level terrain and smaller dunes, while experienced riders showcase their abilities on massive dunes that soar up to 100 feet in height.

There are hundreds of trails in the area, and you can find different trails on most all off-road apps and maps. Google maps provides the easiest route to get from Rock Springs to the dunes.

Directions to Trailhead: From Rock Springs, simply go 12 miles north on State Highway 191 and then turn right (east) onto County Road 4-17/Tri-Territory Loop Road for another 20 miles. Proceed one mile north on the Sand Dunes access road.

## Big Horn National Forest - Sheridan, WY

Trail Rating: East 1 to Hard 7

Trail Type: All types

Trail Length: Over 11,000 acres of dune trails

Approximate Time: As long as you can ride

Best Season: Spring - Fall

Traffic: Moderate to High

Since I cannot list all the trails at this location, here is a QR code from the NFS website that lists the top 95 OHV trails in the area:

With almost 1,200 miles of tracks, you can ride for weeks and never see the same view twice! As part of the Wyoming Trails system, there are 962 back road miles, 188 OHV/ATV trail miles, and 33 single track miles in the Big Horn.

There are literally hundreds of locations and sights to view in the Bighorn Mountains when exploring with your off-road vehicle, including a variety of wildlife, waterfalls, picturesque vistas, mountain lakes and streams, and historic sites.

If you want more fun in this area, you can find over 90 different Bighorn trails at the Bighorn National Forest website by searching "*Bighorn National Forest OHV Trail Riding.*"

Here are a few of the more popular trails in the area:

- **Hazleton Kaycee Loop - Buffalo, WY**

Trail Rating: Easy 2

Trail Type: Loop

Trail Length: 100

Approximate Time: 8 hours

Best Season: Late Spring - Fall

Traffic: Low

Trailhead Coordinates: 43.648145, -106.620635

This easy off-road trip is absolutely amazing! Keep in mind that the area is quite isolated, and you might go about 50 miles without encountering another soul.

Some parts of these middle miles can be a bit rough, but they don't quite reach any serious difficulty level, so fear no, this is just a beautiful, fun, easy drive that anyone can enjoy.

Directions to Trailhead: From Kaycee travel south on WY-196 S/Nolan Ave/Old Hwy 87 for 4 miles. Then turn right onto WY-196 S and after ½ mile turn right (west) onto Ttt Rd.

This loop takes you along the southern part of the Bighorn Mountains. You can find out more about this trail on Gaia GPS.

- **Little Goose and Bighorn OHV Loop - Story, WY**

  Trail Rating: Moderate 4 - 5

  Trail Type:  Out and Back

  Trail Length: 21 Miles

  Approximate Time: 4 Hours

  Best Season: Late Spring - Fall

  Traffic: Low

  Trailhead Coordinates: 44.589573, -107.125255

  This trail goes through the Little Goose area of the Bighorn Mountains. There are many off-roading trails in this area. The road goes around Park Reservoir on the west side of the loop.

  A little further south, many stock 4x4 drivers go to Bighorn Reservoir because the road gets narrower and harder after this point. You'll go through dense evergreen woods, cross some huge meadows, and cross a number of creeks on the east side of the loop. Also, on the east side, keep an eye out for a sign for Little Goose Falls. There are secondary trails and designated ATV trails (ORV permit needed) on both sides of this route that go for more than 50 miles.

  Directions to trailhead: From Sheridan, travel south on WY-332 S/Big Horn Ave for 5 miles.  At the intersection with Coffeen Ave, turn right onto WY-335 S for 9.3 miles. The road will become Red Grade Rd/Co Rd 26 for 4.7 miles.  Then turn left onto Evans Rd/Co Rd 75 for 2.4 miles.  Once you arrive at the Little Goose Campground, you are at the trailhead.

  There are several basic campsites along the trail.  You can find this trail on OnX Offroad, and variations of this trail on AllTrails+, and Trailforks.

## Phillips Ridge Trail - Wilson, WY

Trail Rating: Moderately Hard 5-6

Trail Type: Out and Back

Trail Length: 21 Miles

Approximate Time: 9 hours

Best Season: Summer - Fall

Traffic: Moderate

Trailhead Coordinates: 43.50532, -110.92737

Try out this out-and-back trail is a route that is generally considered to be fairly difficult, and it takes several hours to complete. Despite the fact that this path is a popular destination for 4X4s, as well as mountain bikers, birdwatching, and hiking, you may still find some peace and quiet here during the less busy periods of the day. This trail offers some beautiful vistas, and exploring the trail with friends or family can be a fun experience.

Directions to trailhead: From Jackson, WY travel west on US-191 S/US-26 W/US-89 S. Turn right (north) onto WY-22/Teton Pass Hwy for 9.5 miles. Turn right (north) Forest Rd 30972.

You can find the map, photos, and more about this trail on the AllTrails+ app.

## Blacktail ORV Trails - Sundance, WY

Trail Rating: Easy 2 - Moderate 6

Trail Type: Varies

Trail Length: Varies

Approximate Time: Varies

Best Season: Mid-May - November

Traffic: Moderate - High

Trailhead Coordinates: 44.57912, -104.48641

Off-roading in the Black Hills National Forest is an exciting ATV/OHV/Motorcycle recreation area. The rugged terrain and beautiful scenery make for a unique setting for off-roading fans to explore. With hundreds of miles of marked trails, the Blacktail and the Bighorn Mountains are a great place for off-road fans. Jeeps and full-size SUVs are prohibited on some of these trails because of width issues.

## Ogden Creek Trail System

Trail Rating: Easy 2 - Moderate 6

Trail Type: Varies

Trail Length: Varies

Approximate Time: Varies

Best Season: May - November

Traffic: Moderate

Trailhead Coordinates: 44.443082, -104.348846

Four OHV trails are accessible from the Ogden Creek Motorized Trailhead southeast of Warren Peak. The trailhead is well located for riders in the area and is around ten miles away from Sundance. Vehicles wider than 50" are not permitted.

Directions to trailhead: From Sundance (Exit 185 of Interstate 90), take US14 northwest for about 0.9 mile to Crook County 63, National Forest Service Road (NFSR) 838, to reach the Ogden Creek Motorized Trailhead. To reach NFSR 839.1, continue north (right) on Warren Peak Road (NFSR 838) for 6.2 miles. After making an easterly (right) turn onto NFSR 839.1, continue for about 1.5 miles until the road comes to a stop at the trailhead.

## A Few Last Words About Wyoming

The backroads of Wyoming will take you away from the paved roads and into the wilderness, where you will discover breathtaking scenery, natural features, historical sites, and an abundance of wildlife. There are hundreds of challenging four-wheel  drive roads and off-road vehicle parks that can be utilized to move further away from the typical tourist destinations.

Off-roading is an activity that is both thrilling and daring, and it is popular in the Northern Rocky Mountains. Those who are interested in off-roading will find that the rough terrain and breathtaking scenery present them with an environment that is both distinctive and challenging to explore. Thousands of miles of authorized trails can be found in Wyoming, making them a paradise for people who enjoy off-roading opportunities.

There are a variety of off-road trails in Wyoming, offering a range of experiences from scenic drives to challenging routes. The paths provide breathtaking views of the beautiful surroundings, taking you through lush forests, expansive meadows, and rugged mountainous terrain. Off-roading is an exhilarating adventure, thanks to the challenging terrain and this state's variety of topographical elements.

# Chapter 10:

# Final Thoughts

**Trail Like a Pro, Drive Like a Legend**

Now, I know you're itching to tackle those legendary off-road trails like a boss. But always remember to **stay updated on trail conditions, follow trail etiquette, and put safety first.** After all, a great off-road memory is one where you navigated like a pro and came home unscathed.

**Preservation through Appreciation**

As you rev up your off-road spirit, savoring the raw beauty of the Mountain West, remember this: *the more we cherish these wild playgrounds, the more they'll continue to awe and inspire generations to come.* By becoming the best off-road enthusiast you can be, you're not just conquering terrains; you're safeguarding Mother Nature's wonders for future thrill-seekers.

**Keep Exploring, Keep Smiling**

So, as you take on your own off-road trails, try to remember: *off-roading isn't just about the trails we conquer; it's about the memories we create, the connections we forge, and the love we share for this breathtaking wilderness.* So keep exploring, keep smiling, and let every off-road adventure be a tribute to the untamed beauty that surrounds us.

## Taking the Wheel: Your Next Steps

With the map spread out on the hood and the world at your tires, what's next? It's simple: **start planning your next adventure.** Use the insights gained from this book to chart a course that challenges you, excites you, and, above all, leads you to discover the beauty and thrill of the off-road experience. Remember, in the world of off-roading, the journey is as important as the destination. So, whether it's trying out a new trail, tweaking your rig for better performance, or simply sharing your experiences with fellow enthusiasts, keep having fun while safely pushing the limits.

Of course, the road doesn't end here. **Further exploration is needed**, both on the ground and in our understanding of the intimate dance between nature and machine. As much as we've covered, there's always another trail, another modification, and another challenge waiting just beyond the next ridge.

## The Call to Adventure

Let this book be another step off the beaten path as you take on the trails of the Rocky Mountain West. Keep your spirits high, your wheels spinning, and remember—the best views come after the hardest climbs.

As you embark on your next thrilling journey, I want to share two quotes that I believe truly capture the essence of our mutual passion for exploration and new experiences:

"Sometimes the road you travel doesn't lead to the destination you had hoped for. But if you can look back on the trip and smile, then it's worth it." Anonymous.

184

"There are no wrong turns when you take the golden chance of traveling the less-traveled roads." Susan Magsamen.

Drive safe, explore responsibly, and never stop seeking the thrill of the trail. Happy off-roading!

# Free Maps & Other Items

**CLICK ON THIS QR CODE TO GET ACCESS TO FREE BOOKS, MAPS, AND MUCH MORE!**

# About The Author

Steven Lee is widely known and respected in the entertainment industry for his work as a feature film producer. Having an impressive portfolio of over 40 movies and TV series, he has proven himself as a seasoned professional in the field.

His talent for storytelling shines through in the fact that three of his screenplays have been successfully produced and distributed on major platforms like Disney, Amazon, and Netflix.

Steven's love for writing extends beyond his work in the film industry. His passion for writing has taken him on a journey through different genres, from fiction to non-fiction. Steven's passion for his craft shines through in everything he does, from crafting intricate narratives to sharing his insights through articles and books.

Steven clearly understands the significance of enjoying life and embracing a lighthearted approach, as evidenced by his personal interests. He frequently highlights the value of humor and levity in both his work and personal life, always putting a funny twist on things.

Steven is someone who truly enjoys the great outdoors and appreciates its beauty. He thoroughly enjoys immersing himself his love for adventure as he is often found out venturing to the nearby mountains for off-roading and exploration. Steven's deep appreciation for the outdoors fuels his creativity and serves as a wellspring of inspiration for his stories.

# References

- A grand tour of the San Rafael Swell. (n.d.). Visit Utah. https://www.visitutah.com/Articles/A-Grand-Tour-of-the-San-Rafael-Swell

- AllTrails: trail Guides & maps for hiking, camping, and running. (n.d.). AllTrails.com. https://www.alltrails.com/?ref=header

- Amy. (2021, September 1). Off-Road hand signals. Bullhide 4x4. https://bullhide4x4.com/off-road-hand-signals/

- Apps - Trails offroad. (n.d.). https://www.trailsoffroad.com/apps

- Arapeen OHV Trail. (n.d.). UTAH TRAILS. https://www.utahatvtrails.org/

- Arizona Peace Trail spur Salome to Harquahala Peak, Arizona : Off-Road Map, Guide, and Tips | onX Offroad. (n.d.). onX Offroad. https://www.onxmaps.com/offroad/trails/us/arizona/arizona-peace-trail-spur-salome-to-harquahala-peak

- Arizona Peace Trail West. (n.d.). Alltrails.com. Retrieved February 19, 2024, from https://www.alltrails.com/trail/us/arizona/arizona-peace-trail-west

- Avenza Maps | the #1 digital map store. (n.d.). https://store.avenza.com/?campaignid=10221828697&adgroupid=102940455500&adid=453328850375&gad_source=1&gclid=CjwKCAiA8sauBhB3EiwAruTRJk4t1P oUgBt_4UPSCP8bZyb9sRlR1L3B6DLlq2F_yvc4Ho4Q d_VDTBoCLUsQAvD_BwE

187

- Azpt. (n.d.). Arizona Peace Trail. Arizona Peace Trail. https://arizonapeacetrail.org/

- BackCountry Navigator PRO — BackCountry Navigator. (n.d.). BackCountry Navigator. https://www.backcountrynavigator.com/backcountry-navigator-pro3

- Backway to Crown King — AZOFFROAD.NET. (n.d.). AZOFFROAD.NET. https://azoffroad.net/backway-to-crown-king

- Benbow Jeep Trail, Montana : Off-Road Map, Guide, and Tips | ONX OffRoad. (n.d.). onX Offroad. https://www.onxmaps.com/offroad/trails/us/montana/benbow-jeep-trail

- Best off road driving trails in Lake Havasu City. (n.d.-a). AllTrails.com. https://www.alltrails.com/us/arizona/lake-havasu-city/off-road-driving

- Best off road driving trails in Lake Havasu City. (n.d.-b). AllTrails.com. https://www.alltrails.com/us/arizona/lake-havasu-city/off-road-driving

- Best Off Road GPS App for Android - ATV, Dirt Bike & UTV Trail Maps | ONX. (2023, October 24). onX Offroad. https://www.onxmaps.com/offroad/app/features/android-gps-trail-maps

- bigrigmedia. (2019, December 12). The Best Off&#x2d;Roading in Las Cruces | Hacienda RV REeort. Hacienda RV Resort. https://www.haciendarv.com/the-best-off-roading-in-las-cruces/

- Blacktail ORV Trails Adventure. (n.d.). https://www.devilstowercountry.com/travel-stories/78-blacktail-atv-trails-adventures-in-crook-county

- Bound, O. (2024, February 11). Overland bound - Off-Road mapping and trip planning. Overland Bound. https://www.overlandbound.com/

- Box Canyon, Arizona : Off-Road Map, Guide, and Tips | ONX OffRoad. (n.d.). onX Offroad. https://www.onxmaps.com/offroad/trails/us/arizona/box-canyon

- Broken Arrow Trail — AZOFFROAD.NET. (n.d.). AZOFFROAD.NET. https://azoffroad.net/broken-arrow-trail

- Bureau of Land Management - Ely District Office. (n.d.). SILVER STATE TRAIL. Nevada Trail Finder. Retrieved March 10, 2024, from https://www.nvtrailfinder.com/trails/trail/silver-state-trail

- Canfield Mountain Trail System. (n.d.). https://www.fs.usda.gov. Retrieved February 24, 2024, from https://www.fs.usda.gov/Internet/FSE_DOCUMENTS/fsm9_018428.pdf

- Cattail Cove/Rovey's Needle - FunTreks. (2020, September 9). FunTreks. https://funtreks.com/off-road-trails/cattail-cove-roveys-needle/

- Challenging trail with many Extra Credits available. - Jeep the USA. (n.d.). https://www.jeeptheusa.com/rocky-gap-30.html

- Cheryl, M. &. (2023, July 6). The Perfect 3-Day Road Trip Through the San Rafael Swell & Central Utah (Helper, Goblin Valley, Price, & More!) - We&#039;re in the Rockies. We're in the Rockies. https://wereintherockies.com/san-rafael-swell/

- Club, L. C. F. W. D. (n.d.). Las Cruces Four Wheel Drive Club. Las Cruces Four Wheel Drive Club.

https://lascrucesfourwheeldriveclub.com/robledo-mountain

- Colorado Activity Centers, Inc. (2023, September 20). 9 amazing 4×4 trails in Colorado | ColoradoInfo. ColoradoInfo | Find Your Colorado. https://www.coloradoinfo.com/blog_post/9-amazing-4x4-trails-in-colorado/

- Drive, D. 4. W., & Drive, D. 4. W. (2023, June 19). What makes off roading at Sand Hollow State Park the next off road mecca. Dixie 4 Wheel Drive. https://dixie4wheeldrive.com/what_makes_off_roading_sand_hollow_state_park_next_off_road_mecca/

- Eagle ATV Tours. (2017, June 24). Off trail etiquette. Retrieved February 27, 2024, from https://eagleatvtours.com/off-road-trail-etiquette/

- Elk Mountain , New Mexico : Off-Road Map, Guide, and Tips | ONX OffRoad. (n.d.). onX Offroad. https://www.onxmaps.com/offroad/trails/us/new-mexico/elk-mountain

- Fabfours.com. (n.d.). OFF ROAD TRAIL ETIQUETTE – STAGING AND PASSING VEHICLES! Retrieved February 27, 2024, from https://fabfours.com/off-road-trail-etiquette-staging-and-passing-vehicles/#:~:text=Above%20all%2C%20whenever%20you%27re,so%20there%20are%20no%20mishaps.

- Fantastic 100 mile off-road trip! - Jeep the USA. (n.d.). https://www.jeeptheusa.com/hazleton-kaycee-loop-gp.html

- FAQ: Is there a universal difficulty rating system for OHV trails? - American Trails. (n.d.). https://www.americantrails.org/resources/faq-is-there-a-universal-difficulty-rating-system-for-ohv-trails

- Find adventures near you, track your progress, share. (n.d.). https://www.bivy.com/adventures/us/utah/north-fork,-fixit-pass,-cane-wash-5279260065398784

- Free Maps. (n.d.). UTAH TRAILS. https://www.utahatvtrails.org/free-maps.html

- Frost, M. (2023, November 29). Pros and Cons of ONX Maps, Trails Offroad VS. Gaia GPS. Tripversed. https://tripversed.com/pros-and-cons-of-onx-maps-trails-offroad-vs-gaia-gps/

- Grand Mesa Jeeping & ATV Trails Map | Colorado Vacation Directory. (n.d.). https://www.coloradodirectory.com/maps/atvgrandmesa.html

- Grand Mesa UncomPahgre and Gunnison National Forests - OHV Riding & Camping:OHV Trail Riding. (n.d.). https://www.fs.usda.gov/activity/gmug/recreation/ohv/?recid=32366&actid=93

- Hamlin, K. (2020a, August 26). Top Off-Road parks and trails by state. OffRoadRacer.com. https://offroadracer.com/top-off-road-sites-by-state/

- Hamlin, K. (2020b, August 26). Top Off-Road parks and trails by state. OffRoadRacer.com. https://offroadracer.com/top-off-road-sites-by-state/

- Holden, C. (2024, February 8). Best Off-Roading Adventures in New Mexico. New Mexico Magazine. Retrieved March 10, 2024, from https://www.newmexicomagazine.org/blog/post/best-off-roading-adventures-new-mexico/

- Idaho, V. (2023, May 31). St. Anthony Sand Dunes | Visit Idaho. Visit Idaho. https://visitidaho.org/things-to-do/natural-attractions/st-anthony-sand-dunes/

- Imogene Pass – near Telluride. (n.d.). https://www.uncovercolorado.com/activities/imogene-pass/

- Intern. (2023, May 2). Best Jeep Off-Roading Destinations in Idaho. Leisure Group Travel. https://leisuregrouptravel.com/best-jeep-off-roading-destinations-in-idaho/#:~:text=The%20beauty%20of%20Idaho%20is,beat%20Idaho%27s%20wealth%20of%20trails.

- Jacoby, N. (2023, May 31). The Ultimate Guide to Airing Down Tires for Off-Roading: Why, When, and how. JACO. https://jacosuperiorproducts.com/blogs/news/the-ultimate-guide-to-airing-down-tires-for-off-roading-why-when-and-how

- Jeffery, & Jeffery. (2023, October 24). Top 8 off road trails in Montana for 4×4 vehicles - Tozalazz. Tozalazz - Best portable 12 volt air compressor for off roading. https://tozalazz.com/top-8-off-road-trails-in-montana-for-4x4-vehicles/

- Killpecker Sand Dunes | Sweetwater County, WY. (n.d.). SWC. https://www.explorewy.com/explore/sightseeing-and-attractions/killpecker-sand-dunes

- Lake Havasu City Convention & Visitors Bureau. (n.d.). Offroad trails. Lake Havasu City. https://www.golakehavasu.com/offroad-driving-routes

- Life, R. (2023, April 10). St Anthony Sand Dunes: Rentals, restrictions, and activities. Rexburg Life. https://rexburglife.com/st-anthony-sand-dunes-rental-restriction-activity/

- Logandale Trails | Bureau of Land Management. (n.d.). https://www.blm.gov/visit/logandale-trails

- Logandale Trails | Moapa Valley OHV Park | Travel Nevada. (2020, December 8). Travel Nevada. https://travelnevada.com/outdoor-recreation/logandale-trails-system/

- Louie Lake Trail | An Epic hiking or Off-Roading route | 10Adventures. (n.d.). 10Adventures. https://www.10adventures.com/hikes/payette-national-forest/louie-lake-trail/

- Lucky lad mine. (n.d.). Mapcarta. https://mapcarta.com/23545250

- Meeker Chamber of Commerce. (n.d.). WAGON WHEEL TRAILS. In Meeker Chamber of Commerce (pp. 3–7). https://meekerchamber.com/wp-content/uploads/2019/07/WagonWheel_2019Guide.pdf

- Metal Masher - Utah Offroad Trail. (n.d.). https://www.trailsoffroad.com/trails/570-metal-masher

- Mike. (2020, December 3). Different Types of Off-Road Suspension Setups &#187; F-O-A | First Over All Off Road Shocks. F-O-A | First Over All off Road Shocks. https://f-o-a.com/types-of-off-road-suspension/

- Moab 4-Wheeling Trails Guide — Discover Moab, Utah. (2023, November 30). Discover Moab, Utah. https://www.discovermoab.com/4-wheeling/

- Montana Mountain - Queen Valley | AZoffroading.com. (2021, October 27). AZoffroading.com. https://azoffroading.com/arizona-trails/queen-valley-montana-mountain/

- Moon Rocks Nevada | OHV Area | Travel Nevada. (2021, November 12). Travel Nevada. https://travelnevada.com/outdoor-recreation/moon-rocks/

- Morrison Jeep Trail - Where2Wheel. (n.d.). https://where2wheel.com/trails/trail/full/539

- Offroad App - Maps and trails for overlanding, 4x4, OHV, and ATV. (n.d.). gaiagps.com. https://www.gaiagps.com/offroad/

- Off-Roading. (n.d.). https://www.bearlodgeresort.com/off-roading

- Off-Roading in Utah | OHV and ATV trails. (n.d.). Visit Utah. https://www.visitutah.com/things-to-do/Motorized-Off-Road#:~:text=One%20of%20Utah's%20top%20off,find%20one%20of%20the%20best.

- OFF-ROADING TRAIL ETIQUETTE GUIDELINES TO FOLLOW. (2020, May 28). Top Lift Pros. Retrieved February 27, 2024, from https://topliftpros.com

- OHV Trails in Meeker, Colorado | Visit Meeker Colorado. (2023, July 10). Visit Meeker Colorado. https://www.visitmeekercolorado.com/adventures/ohv-trails/

- OnX Offroad. (n.d.-a). https://webmap.onxmaps.com/offroad/map/query/44.662838,-115.274059,14.00/overview#14/44.66284/-115.27406

- OnX Offroad. (n.d.-b). https://webmap.onxmaps.com/offroad/map/query/44.55707,-107.15218/overview?id=4f693f92-f013-5610-9848-36d596f4e29c&search=true#15/44.55707/-107.15218

- Ophir Pass – Ophir-Silverton. (n.d.). https://www.uncovercolorado.com/activities/ophir-pass/

- Payette National Forest - OHV Riding & Camping:OHV Trail Riding. (n.d.).

https://www.fs.usda.gov/activity/payette/recreation/ohv/
?recid=26865&actid=93

- Pipestone Off-Highway Vehicle Area | Bureau of Land Management. (n.d.).
https://www.blm.gov/visit/pipestone-th

- Pipestone OHV Area | Southwest Montana. (n.d.).
https://southwestmt.com/blog/pipestone-ohv-area/

- Pony Express Trail, Nevada : Off-Road Map, Guide, and Tips | ONX OffRoad. (n.d.). onX Offroad.
https://www.onxmaps.com/offroad/trails/us/nevada/pony-express-trail

- Riley, E. R. (2019, August 9). Do you have the skills you need to go Off-Road? https://www.faricy.com/. Retrieved February 18, 2024, from https://www.faricy.com/blog/do-you-have-the-skills-you-need-to-go-off-road/

- Road, D. O. (2022, October 4). Places to ride ATVs in Wyoming. DRR USA.
https://www.drrusa.com/post/places-to-ride-atvs-in-wyoming

- Robledo Mountains Off-Highway Vehicle Trail System (BLM) | Las Cruces, NM 88005. (n.d.).
https://www.newmexico.org/listing/robledo-mountains-off-highway-vehicle-trail-system-(blm)/2449/

- Rocky Gap. (n.d.). VegasUnderworld.com.
http://www.vegasunderworld.com/rocky-gap.html

- Russell, F. (2023, February 8). AllTrails versus TrailForks: how do the activity apps stack up against each other? advnture.com.
https://www.advnture.com/features/alltrails-versus-trailforks-how-do-the-activity-apps-stack-up-against-each-other

- Russell, L. (2023, November 30). Off-Roading Guide - Southwest Idaho Travel Association. Southwest Idaho Travel Association. https://www.visitsouthwestidaho.org/off-roading-guide/

- Sand Hollow State Park. (n.d.). Visit Utah. https://www.visitutah.com/Places-To-Go/Parks-Outdoors/Sand-Hollow-State-Park

- Scivally, S. (2023, April 12). Top 10 4x4 trails in Sand Hollow Utah State Park - Tred cred. Tred Cred. https://tredcred.com/top-10-4x4-trails-in-sand-hollow-utah-state-park/

- Severin, T. (2018, March 15). Pony Express Trail a fun, interesting 4WD trip. Badlands 4x4 Training. https://www.4x4training.com/w/pony-express-trail-a-fun-interesting-4wd-trip/

- Shepherd ah nei recreation area. (n.d.). RiderPlanet USA. https://www.riderplanet-usa.com/atv/trails/info/montana_14003/ride_71f1.htm

- Shepherd Ah-Nei OHV Recreation Area. (2022, August 18). https://www.visitmt.com/listings/general/blm-recreation-area/shepherd-ahnei-ohv-recreation-area

- Singler, M. (2023, May 12). ONX Offroad App review: An overlanding essential you won't want to drive without. Gear Patrol. https://www.gearpatrol.com/cars/a42919245/onx-offroad-review/

- St. Anthony Sand Dunes | Bureau of Land Management. (n.d.). https://www.blm.gov/visit/st-anthony-sand-dunes

- Support, I. R. (2023, March 14). Top 5 Off-Roading Trails in Albuquerque - Good Sense RV & Motors blog. Good Sense RV & Motors Blog. https://www.goodsenserv.com/blog/top-5-off-roading-trails-in-albuquerque/#:~:text=New%20Mexico%20has%20countless%20off,easier%20than%20you%27d%20think.

- Surprise Valley Barrel Springs Backcountry Byway | Shastacascade.com. (n.d.). https://www.upstateca.com/account/surprise-valley-barrel-springs-backcountry-byway

- Surprise Valley/Barrel Springs backcountry byway. (2022, July 11). Travel Nevada. https://travelnevada.com/off-roading/surprise-valley-barrel-springs-backcountry-byway/

- The 7 best Trails in the Carbon Corridor Trail System. (n.d.). Visit Utah. https://www.visitutah.com/Articles/7-Best-Off-Roading-Trails-in-Carbon-Corridor

- The best Areas for Off-Roading in Wyoming – TopLift Pros. (2021, October 21). https://topliftpros.com/blogs/news/the-best-areas-for-off-roading-in-wyoming

- The best jeeping trails in New Mexico – TopLift Pros. (2019, July 17). https://topliftpros.com/blogs/news/the-best-jeeping-trails-in-new-mexico

- The Dirt: Beatty to Goldfield Adventure Route | OFF-ROAD Nevada. (n.d.). https://ohv.nv.gov/trails/beatty-to-goldfield-adventure-route#:~:text=The%20Beatty%20to%20Goldfield%20Adventure,cross%2Dcross%20the%20entire%20region.

- The Dirt: Gold Butte National Monument | OFF-ROAD Nevada. (n.d.). https://ohv.nv.gov/trails/gold-butte-national-monument

- The Morrison Jeep Trail – Wyoming. (2021, September 22). Modern Jeeping News & Education. https://modernjeeper.com/the-morrison-jeep-trail-wyoming/

- Tough, C. (2023, August 24). Best UTV / ATV Off-Road Trails in the USA by State. ClearlyTough. https://clearlytough.com/best-utv-off-road-trails-by-state/?utm_source=facebook&utm_medium=engagement&utm_campaign=best_trails&utm_content=2023&fbclid=IwAR2gMKhw2aRNMm0Z5YndT_6TSKtL7O0VQqzNMl67OMRzO6FN1M4OAu53GVk_aem_AabUiXkHDjH7Q2CuMqtseNdrzBDzuI7aXUpW6KARBoZRe-R3qL3atv6FfFU85Es1D9-kDMxgBPAOTS0klW2HVbX_&utm_id=6224417386826&utm_term=6332370479426#arizona

- Travel Montana. (2023, December 20). Reasons to Visit Montana and Yellowstone - From Travel Montana & Yellowstone. Travel Montana & Yellowstone. https://travelmontana.com/why-visit-montana/#:~:text=Montana%20has%20huge%20outdoor%20spaces,Blackfeet%2C%20Kootenai%2C%20Shoshone%2C%20and

- Travel Wyoming. (n.d.). ATV and Off Road Trails are Abundant in Wyoming Wilderness. https://travelwyoming.com/things-to-do/outdoor-adventure/land/atv-off-roading/#:~:text=No%20matter%20your%20preferred%20landscape,and%20Black%20Hills%20national%20forests.

- Utah Arapeen ATV Trail System | Expedition Utah. (n.d.). https://expeditionutah.com/featured-trails/arapeen-ohv-trail-system-courtesty-of-san-pete-county/

- Wagon wheel OHV trails. (n.d.). https://www.wagonwheeltrails.org/home

- Walton, J. (2016, July 17). Benbow Mine Trail for ATV riding. TRAILSOURCE.COM.

https://www.trailsource.com/?type=ATV&id=19424#google_vignette

- World's greatest driving roads. (n.d.-a). Adventure along the remote road to Elk Mountain. World's Greatest Driving Roads. https://www.dangerousroads.org/north-america/usa/9490-elk-mountain-2.html

- World's greatest driving roads. (n.d.-b). Monument ridge. World's Greatest Driving Roads. https://www.dangerousroads.org/north-america/usa/8977-monument-ridge-2.html

- World's greatest driving roads. (n.d.-c). Phantom Canyon Road is a scenic drive in Colorado. World's Greatest Driving Roads. https://www.dangerousroads.org/north-america/usa/4329-phantom-canyon-road.html

- World's greatest driving roads. (n.d.-d). Rocky Gap Road. World's Greatest Driving Roads. https://www.dangerousroads.org/north-america/usa/8558-rocky-gap-road.html

# THE BEGINNING...

.

Made in United States
Troutdale, OR
03/23/2025

29985237R00120